The Books of Nick

The Books of Nick

King Nick

To order additional copies of this book, contact:
Xlibris
1-800-455-039
www.Xlibris.com.au
Orders@Xlibris.com.au
772163

Contents

To my Daughter, oh how I cannot wait to meet you.

The Hearts of Man

The purpose of the gospel is to make bad men good and
good men better, and to change human nature

David O McKay

———⟞⟞⟞∘⟨⟩⟞⟝∘∘⟞⟞⟞———

He who takes offense when no offense is intended is a fool, and he who takes offense when offense is intended is a greater fool

Brigham Young

———————

For the commandment is a lamp; and the law is light;
and reproofs of instruction are the way of life

He is in the way of life that keepeth instruction:
but he that refuseth reproof erreth

Whoso loveth instruction loveth knowledge:
but he that hateth reproof is brutish

Poverty and shame shall be to him that refuseth instruction:
but he that regardeth reproof shall be honoured

A reproof entereth more into a wise man
than an hundred stripes into a fool

The rod and reproof give wisdom

Proverbs

King Solomon

He that overcometh shall inherit all things; and I
will be his God, and he shall be my Son
Revelations 21

Heavenly Father loves you as you are, but that does
not mean that he wants to leave you as you are.

He wants us to become like him, in heart, mind, spirit and character.

God's ultimate purpose is our progress
D. Todd Christofferson

Thine arrows are sharp in the heart of the king's
enemies whereby the people fall under thee
Psalm 45

———⌇⌇ೲ⌇ೲ⌇———

A Heavenly Mother

O my preciousness I wish you well,
As you embark on your journey through that living hell.
Know that we will be watching you,
And doing our best to help you in all that you do.
Remember that we will respect the choices you make,
But if you wish to return to us you must learn our ways.
I wish you the best and I pray you will find,
The straight and narrow way,
That leads to a life like mine.

We have Heavenly Parents. Our highest aspiration is to be like them.

A Heavenly Father

Oh my children look at you all!
I wish that you all could see!
All the wonders that I have in store!
For you in Eternity!
But for the ones who are proven true!
How more blessed they will be!
For everything that I have will be theirs!
If they will only promise me!
That they will keep my commandments!
And strive to be!
Of one heart and mind with me!
My Spirit I will send to guide the way!

All you have to do is turn your every thought unto me!

It is mentally rigorous to strive to look unto him in every thought. But when we do, our doubts and fears flee.
Russell M. Nelson

———⟋⟍⟋⟍⟋⟍⟋⟍———

Our Older Brother The Saviour

Oh no! What have you done!
You've accumulated a debt you cannot pay!
Heavenly Father please send me!
For I can see no other way!
If I don't go they will be lost!
And they will all be gone away!
I understand all that I will have to endure!
But I love my brethren so much!
Send Me Father! I will go!
And show to them the way!
That if they choose to follow!
They may live with thee again!

We rejoice in all the Saviour has done for us. He has made it possible for each of us to gain our salvation and exaltation.
Quentin L Cook

———⟋⟍⟋⟍⟋⟍⟋⟍———

The Humble Seeker of Happiness

The wisest man alive is the humble seeker of happiness.
He seeks after a treasure that cannot be bought.
It is a prize that over many wars are fought.
To have this gift, men give their lives.
In order to keep it, many are willing to die.
But greater is there than the happiness of man,
That which I speak off is God's great plan.
His teachings enable us to learn of a happiness divine,
That which God enjoys yea a love so fine.
Kings would give up all that they had,
If they knew the joy that God has.
He who has tasted of it cannot forget,
It will be all that now fills his head.
How do I get more?
How do I keep it?
Please God teach me, how do I receive it?
Master the commandments Son that's what they are for,
And not just some, but learn them all.
My Spirit I will send to teach you how,
If you would only ask me now.
The more you apply the happier you will be,
Come on and try me and you will see!

Happiness is the objective of our existence.
Joseph Smith

The Philosopher Kings

They love wisdom!
They love to learn!
Improvement and progression,
Of this they yearn!
What is my ignorance!
What is stopping me!
From improving and progressing,
This gives my life its meaning.
Don't forget to take everything you read
To the Holy Ghost for polishing and cleaning!

A wise man will hear and will increase learning.
Proverbs 1:5

The Truly Penitent

Who can rejoice too much in the Lord!
From whom the river of mercy rains!
I cannot say the smallest part!
Of that which I now feel!
He rescued my Soul from the deepest pain!
He withheld the sword of Justice!
Sentencing me not to an Eternal despair!
He clenched me with his Love!
And showed to me the ways above!
Taught to me the ways to salvation!

Now my brethren can Ye harken!
What natural man is there?
That knoweth these things?
None!
Only the truly penitent this song can sing!

What natural man is there that knoweth these things? I say unto
you, there is none that knoweth these things, save it be the penitent.
Alma 26:21

The Loving Husband

Ah my Wife! You are my Life!
Without you life would not be the same!
You are the spice that adds to life!
It's wonderful tastes!!
The smell of your beauty!
And the taste of your scent!
Is what makes my life magnificent!
So with all my heart!
I have you to thank!

The wedding is the planting, but the marriage is the season.
John Bytheway

The Loving Wife

Oh my King! My bells you ring!
As to me your heart sings!
I love you my dear! I always will!
You are my well of serene!
Can you see the gleam in my eye!
You cause me with happiness to cry!
At night when you sleep!
I gaze at you!
And pray that you will always love me too!

Marriage is the most trusting step in any human relationship.
Its a real act of faith. The very nature of the endeavour requires
that you hold on to each other as tightly as you can and jump.
Jeffrey R Holland

The Priest

Ah my wife! Let me show you!
Just how much Heavenly Father loves you!
Through my eyes! I hope you can see!
This love that is in me! He gave to me!
I hope that I can show you throughout our life!
A taste of Heaven for being my wife!
I hope and pray that you can see!
Just how much I do appreciate thee!
I hope and pray that I am worthy!

To receive Fathers counsel!
On how to lead thee!
And that together we may raise!
A righteous posterity!
And that we may be!
Exalted together for Eternity!

Your wife is your equal. In marriage neither partner is
superior nor inferior to the other. You walk side by side as
a son and a daughter of God. She is not to be demeaned
or insulted but should be respected and loved.
Thomas S Monson

The Priestess

Oh my Priest! How is it that!
You can hear! Heavenly Father talk back!
What does he say? How does he sound?
And doth he speak with a smile or a frown?
Where does he live? What does he do?
Did the answer to this he leave any clues?
How is it that he always knows what to do?
And why is it that he reveals it to you?
Thank you my Priest! Thank you my King!
For living your life worthily!
That this song I may sing!

For a man to operate independent of or without regard
to the feelings and counsel of his wife in governing
the family is to exercise unrighteous dominion.
Howard W Hunter

The Loving Father

Come my son, I want to teach you,
Everything I know so when you grow old,
You will know of the love I hold.
I want to see you achieve your dreams,
It would mean so much to me,
To see my son succeed.
You can do it I know you can!
But know that no matter what happens,
Of just how proud I am!

Father is the noblest title a man can be given. It is more than
a biological role it signifies a leader, an exemplar, a confidant,
a teacher, a hero, a friend and ultimately a perfect being.
Robert L Backman

The Loving Mother

Oh my darling it's okay,
Come tell mummy what happened again.
What can I do to comfort you?
It's all my fault I wasn't there to protect you.
Just remember who loves you the most!
Come here my baby, let me hold you close.

There is no role in life more essential and more
Eternal than that of motherhood.
M Russell Ballard

The Christ Centred Mind

Filled with truth and understanding,
His ways are never over bearing.
Except when the Gospel you do deny,
Or when you try to sneak a lie.
His love is never too demanding,
Unless he sees that your not even trying,
And he loves you too much to just sit and watch you dying.
His heart is so forgiving,
Even when a grudge you hold,
And anger at him and he even knows.
Peace fills his countenance and the air around him,
The fragrance of happiness seems to spawn from within.
How did this man become to be,

Someone so Great and Mighty,
So strong and bold,
A Possessor of such self control.

It begins with baptism by one with proper authority.
And then by the laying on of hands
The Holy Ghost you will receive,
Who whispers to you,
That which you need to change the most.
A broken heart and a contrite spirit,
Shows that you want to learn.
Study hard the Holy scriptures,
And listen to his appointed leaders.
Learn by the Spirit to keep not one but all,
The commandments that will save you from a mighty fall.
Line upon line, precept upon precept,
The Holy Ghost will teach you
Until you grasp all that Heaven asks,
And become perfect, just as he asks.

And he gave some apostles and some prophets and
some evangelists and some pastors and teachers.
For the perfecting of the saints, for the work of the
ministry, for the edifying of the body of Christ.
Till we all come in the unity of the faith, and of the
knowledge of the Son of God, unto a perfect man, unto
the measure of the stature of the fulness of Christ.
Ephesians 4:11-13

The Pure In Heart

The devil and his angels he battles everyday.
In the war in heaven he fought them all the way.
Now they seek to take away his eternal prize,
Their only desire is for that man to die.
Everyday they try, to tempt him and lead him astray.
Everyday does he pray to conquer all their tricky ways.
Heavenly helpers answer his call,
And help him through his stumbles and falls.

No one at any age is immune from Satans influence.
Kevin W Pearson

Pray always that you may come off conqueror.
D&C 10:5

A Few Hearts Apart

Fools concern themselves with the thoughts of the ignorant,
While Princes and Kings will bask themselves in the Spirit of God!
That they may learn of his knowledge and wisdom!
And of his thoughts and ways!
The wise seek after his righteousness!
And the Great seek after his Love!

The fear of the Lord is the beginning of knowledge,
but fools despise wisdom and instruction.
Proverbs 1:7

———⟶∿∿o⟋⟍o⟋⟋⟍o⟋o∿∿⟵———

The Patriot

Friends! Brothers! Countrymen!
Praise to our God for our many liberties!
Who saved our Souls from captivity!
And delivered us from the wrath of tyrants and dictators!
We must not lax or take them for granted!
For greedy men will always seek!
To take control of the humble and meek!
Stand with me now! For we are at war!
For as I speak!
Evil men are conspiring against us!
Behind closed doors!

Moroni could have pointed out many factors that led to
the destruction of the people, but. he singled out the secret
combinations. The church today has singled out the greatest
threat as the godless conspiracy. There is no conspiracy
in the Book of Mormon - it is a conspiracy fact.
Ezra Taft Benson

———⟶∿∿o⟋⟍o⟋⟋⟍o⟋o∿∿⟵———

The Humble Homeless Man

If he had a dollar he would give you half,
Because he knows what it feels like to starve.
The pain he has suffered he desires for no one,
Some of these are Fathers most cherished son's.
If he could he would bear your burdens,
A brother of Christ, a man without price.
Forged in the crucible of mortality,
He is likely to be a God for all of Eternity.

We often think of charity as an action. But I
think of charity as a state of the Heart.
Elaine Dalton

The Broken Hearted

They may be broken but throw them not away,
For their only desire is to live again the youth of their days.
When everything was happy,
And they had not a care in the world.
Before they were bitten,
By the devil and his angels.
The medicines of man can help them not.
But the succour of Christ,
Lies their only chance at a renewed life.

Through the great miracle of the Atonement of Jesus Christ,
He will give your heart back to you healed and whole.
Jeffrey R Holland

———✿———

The Big Hearted

Often their hearts are bigger than their pockets,
Because along the way, they gave everything away!
These generous souls are one in a billion,
It is a shame that there are not more of the same!

Charity is not a duty but a Joy!
Joseph W Sitati

———✿———

The Treasure Hunter

Can you see the glimmer in his eye?
Can you see an honesty that cannot lie?
What is he looking for? Do you know?
He looks like he's found a pirate ship full of gold!
What is he looking for? I don't know,
"Excuse me sir? What do you see?"
"Could you tell me? Could you show me?"
"Certainly boy! The treasures of Eternity!"

"Can you this not see???"
"They are right here in front of you!"
"For any man to grab!"
"Here take this book! And in it there is a map!"

(The Book of Mormon – Another documented record
of Jesus Christ of his visit to ancient America)

———✶———

Social Correctness The Nice Guy

Is he really nice?
I know he comes across that way,
But can you not see him thinking twice?
His heart and his mouth don't speak the same language,
He's stuck in the middle of an emotional sandwich,
Torn between how he really feels,
And the fear of offending or being disliked,
So he ends up saying what he thinks you'll like.
Smiles and tries so hard to be polite,
Until your at last out of his sight.
And when your back is turned,
He gets frustrated and says things that
would make your stomach churn.
Come unto God!
And allow him to work out your every thought!

The Lord sees weaknesses differently than rebellion. When
the Lord speaks of weaknesses it is always with Mercy.

Richard G Scott

—⟡⟐⟡⟐⟡⟐⟡—

The Weird

Having a moment of weakness?
Need some advice?
Trying to be better?
Need to talk about a vice?
Well from these people you should run!
For they will only laugh at you and make fun.
Not very pleasant to be around,
They like to kick you when your already down.
I think their brain has been wired the wrong way,
Possibly due to insecurities I'd say.
For them again the antidote is God!
Ask him to rewire your brain again,
According to the Iron Rod.
Compassion and love for them is queer,
For they were hurt, by someone else who at them jeered.
So try to understand that it's not their fault,
It could also just be the way that they were taught.

The Church is like a big hospital, and we are all sick in our own way.
We must be tolerant while others work on their individual illnesses;
we must also be kind, patient, supportive and understanding.
As God encourages us to keep on trying, he expects us to also
allow others the space to do the same, at their own pace.
Dale G Renlund

—⟡⟐⟡⟐⟡⟐⟡—

Minions Of The Devil

If they saw a fat kid trying to loose weight,
These are the type that would tempt him with cake,
Hoping in their hearts that he would take.
It pleases them to see another fail,
They get satisfaction from telling everyone the tale:
"See! He lies! He said he was dieting! But he is just lying!"
"No my dear, I am trying. It is so hard, at times I feel like crying."

For thou, Lord, hast mad me glad through thy work,
I will triumph in the works of thy hands.
O Lord, how great are thy works! And thy thoughts are very deep.
A brutish man knoweth not, neither doth a fool understand this.
Psalms 92:4-6

The Gentleman of Babylon

He will deceive you while he wears a smile,
Will appear as caring but really he is just daring.
From his mouth a thick sludge pours.
As he speaks, his countenance tells all.
His tongue will flatter you when you can hear,
But when he thinks no one is looking or is near,
To his true self, he will revert,
The one that laid dormant, almost inert.
Greedy is he and cunning as well,
Entrapped by the everlasting chains of hell.

He will pretend to be your friend,
Just to come across as a gentleman.
For image is everything to he,
And desires himself an idol to be.
Die he would if he knew you could see,
Through the charade that he wants you to believe.

Faithful are the wounds of a friend, but the
kisses of an enemy are deceitful.
Proverbs 27:6

The Tell You What You Want To Hear

Answer you they will, true or untrue,
They will tell you, whatever they want to.
To get what they want, they will say,
Anything and everything, whatever it takes.
These people are the most cunning of all.
Their souls are entrapped and chained.
They are students of the Gospel of hell,
Educated in the arts of deceit and trickery,
They spend their days, refining this well.
Tangled deep in the devils web, escape will be hard,
For the devil does not easily, like to let go.

They speak vanity every one with his neighbour, with
flattering lips and with a double heart do they speak.
Psalm 12:2

The Back Biter

Evil are they in their secret ways,
You can tell by the things that they say.
Both sides of the field do they play,
Stirring every body up in every way.
Their complaints of others they state as fact,
And then do the same thing, behind your back.
So beware the back biters,
And remember, they are dangerous.

The Lord shall cut off all flattering lips, and
the tongue that speakers proud things.
Psalm 12:3

The Back Biter 2

Perhaps the most common of sins,
How easy it is to have a go at him,
While his back is turned and cannot hear,

I suppose it would be better than if he were near.
So I'll just fire away everything I have,
After all it's my point of view,
So therefore yes! It must be true!
Beware my 'friend',
For when your back is turned,
I will speak evil and unkind things of you.

Who have said, with our tongue will we prevail,
our lips are our own: who is lord over us?
Psalm 12:4

———⁓ᵥₙₒₑᵗₒₒₑₒₒᵥₙ———

Mr Insincere

Oh how they look at you, with laughter in their heart,
Oh you poor boy, you haven't a clue,
Of what I really think of you.
Because I like to smile and play it cool,
There is no way that you can see,
As thou art nothing, but a fool.
How silly do they look
When they try so hard,
Pretending to be, sincere, kind and dear.
But to the truth they have no clue,
Of the obviousness of their parade.
They believe that others they can fool,
Because they think that they are smarter than you.
So an effort do they pour into this masquerade,
Until cursed are they and that way do they stay.

And if men come unto me I will show unto them their weakness.
I give unto men weakness that they may be humble; and my
grace is sufficient for all men that humble themselves before
me; for if they humble themselves before me, and have faith in
me, then will I make weak things become strong unto them.
Ether 12:27

The Light Supporters

They carry the flag which boldly bears the name,
We are the light and for this we will fight!
But upon reception of the slightest degree,
Of Spiritual light sent directly from the Eternities,
They get annoyed that they have to squint,
As their eyes try to adjust to what light really is.
Light is truth and truth is light,
This is its only definition.

Through the companionship of the Holy Ghost, the light
of the gospel will cut through confusion and despair.
Kim B Clark

The Agree'ers

They listen to reply but not to understand,
As they nod their heads and agree with you,
While in their hearts they think:
"Oh you poor fool!"
Waiting and waiting for their turn to pounce,
Like a cat to a rat
Hahaha I have you now!
The urge to contend is all they know,
Their nodding in agreement is just for show,
So they don't appear rude, they pretend to agree,
Then when your sentence is finished.
"HAHA FINALLY!"
"It is my turn now! I hope you are ready!"
"I will cut you asunder now surely and gently!"

Contention in our families drives the Spirit of the Lord
away. It also drives many of our family members away.
Ezra Taft Benson

Social Life In Babylon

Social anxiety what a disease,
How this should give you reason to go to your knees.
To cry unto God, Oh won't you please,
Teach me how to be, forever at ease.
Why do I feel that everybody, I must please,

Or when devils flatter me, I need believe.
Why do I feel that I should be polite,
Even unto those that I don't like.
Why do I feel that I should shun the fight,
Even when I know that I am right.
Teach me dear God to be Great like you!
That I may speak boldly of that which is true.

Spiritual light rarely comes to those who merely sit in
darkness waiting for someone to flip a switch.
Dieter F Uchtdorf

The Unforgiving

Destined for a life of misery and bitterness,
The sweet nectar of the fullness of joy they will never know,
For upon their souls, satan has a mighty hold.
More than often those whom they hold a grudge toward,
Never gave them, not even a second thought.
But day after day they hold on to the hot coal
Burning only themselves because of the grudge that they hold.

Somehow forgiveness accomplishes miracles
that can happen in no other way.
Gordon B Hinckley

The Materialist

Oh a new iPhone I must have that,
It's half a mil thinner boy I like that!
It's the latest, if I have it, I will be the greatest!
Everybody will love me if I have that!
It would make my life better in every way!
I have to have it, I just must!
No sir no! This isn't lust.

We all need some stuff, and most stuff is neither good nor bad
in and of itself. Neither is most advertising unless it is trying
to sell us something harmful or has inappropriate content. But
over time the incessant drone of materialism can influence our
attitudes and thoughts and cause us to forget the Lord and his
commandments, as well as our true selves so we must be on guard.
David A Edwards

The Carnal Mind

Like the pig that loves to roll in the mud,
The carnal mind thirsts after lust.
Day by day the need grows strong,
Until one day the love is all gone.
All that remains in this man's mind,
Is how he and himself can have a good time.
All that was good now no more,
All his love, inwardly does he pour.
The desire to please and need another,

Replaced with greed and selfishness doth smother.
The soul eventually becomes dark,
And can no longer tell love and lust apart.
Oh how sore the curse,
Of he who giveth up all of his gold,
For only a little bit of dirty mould.

Pornography is the quickest way to Hell,
The Hell of not being able to tell love and lust apart.

———◦◦◦◦◦◦◦◦◦———

The Haters

They love to hate,
Especially the greats.
Jealous of others success,
They hibernate themselves into a recess,
Shouting curses at those
Who mustered fortunes untold.
Labelling them as selfish or even greedy,
When they themselves are just plain stupid and lazy.
And in their hearts they desire to be just as rich,
But have not the brains nor the itch.
Nor do they turn their all to God
That thereby they may be taught.

Thy shalt not covert thy neighbours.

———◦◦◦◦◦◦◦◦◦———

The Babylonian

These poor poor people.
Unless they come before their God,
With a broken heart and a contrite spirit and sins declaring,
A fullness of joy they will never know.
For the chance at repentance is more precious than gold.
And the prize of forgiveness more valuable than wealth untold.
To be free from sin! Oh what a prize!
To be able to stand upright and not have to hide!
Weighed down no more by the shackles of sin!
You can stand before your maker as tall as him!

The moment we decide to try again, the
Atonement of Christ can help us.
Dale G Renlund

The Prideful Know-it-all

The great destroyer of clear thought,
Pride leaves its victims in a fog.
They think they know it all but fail to see,
The lack of logic behind their reasoning.

Pride is concerned with who is right. Humility
is concerned with what is right.
Ezra Taft Benson

The Terrified

Of the world he is terrified.
Been a victim and vilified.
But of all this he tries so hard to hide,
Because it hurts him so much and so deep inside.
But all the denying just makes it worse,
He ends up numbing himself with lies,
By telling himself that he is alright.
To the atonement he should turn,
And pray for power to within him burn.
If he seeks, he will find,
All the keys, to his needs.

Repentance is the key with which we can unlock
the prison from inside. We hold that key within
our hands, and agency is ours to use it.
Boyd K Packer

The Hysterical

These poor souls, they are out of control,
How to act for themselves they do not know.
Miserable are they yet they cannot see,
The Devils that torment them incessantly.
Causing them to laugh without probable cause,
Even when the situation is far from funny.
Hahaha Hehehe,
Oh how sad they are to see.

The laughter of the world is merely loneliness trying to reassure itself.
Neal A Maxwell

The Hyenas

They laugh at anything, anyone and nearly everything,
Little reason is needed for excessive celebrating.
The Gospel to them is merely entertaining.
Hahahahehehe, these poor people are so sad to see.
Loud stupid insincere laughter is the only way they know,
Or secret cowardly anger, their expressions are but for show.
Cunning are they, it is so sad to see,
Their mannerisms and hearts, are so far from he.
But instead in the gravity of each other do they dwell,
Peer pressure forcing them into the slavery of hell.
Puffing up each other's hearts, with honour and glory,
They are addicted to the swell.

The moment of gravest danger is when there is so
little light that darkness seems normal.
Neal A Maxwell

Mr Personal Relations

How he tries everybody to please,
And how he manages this with ease.
But so many lies does he have to remember,
Worried that he will be discovered as a pretender.
Careful is he not to offend,
But this he does by putting in the truth,
A bit of a bend.
A little white lie,
Surely nobody will die?
I am causing nobody harm,
It's not my fault that everybody is dumb.
And besides, I'm just having a little fun.

A lying tongue hateth those that are afflicted by
it; and a flattering mouth worketh ruin.
Proverbs 26:28

———

The Judgement Seat Takers

They cross a line that no man should cross,
They hold a man to his sins,
After he has been forgiven by God.
Oh dear me! I'd hate to be them!
Firstly the Laws of Mercy and Justice they do not understand.
Secondly God remembers no more these sins,
So they are bearing false witness strongly against him.
Thirdly they are insulting the Atonement paid,

By condemning this man that God forgave.
Fourthly well,
They might as well ring hell and make a reservation,
I sure hope they can stand the smell.
Serves you right is all I can say,
It's your own fault for picking on him.
Yes it is this serious a sin.

Decrease the belief in God, and you increase the numbers of those
who wish to play at being God by being "society's supervisors".
Such "supervisors" deny the existence of divine standards, but are
very serious about imposing their own standards on society.
Neal A Maxwell
As if they were God.

The People Pleaser

It is impossible to please everybody,
But still he tries.
This poor soul is likely,
To do this until he dies.
Anxiously existing as he seeks out new ways,
To keep everybody happy
Throughout all of his days.

The true badge of courage is overcoming the fear of men.
Lynn G Robbins

The Alcoholic

It would be better for a woman to be alone,
Than to put up with a man who doesn't want to go home.
He sits at the bar drinking late,
And never takes his wife out on dates.
Why do you do this man!
For God's sake!

It is not for kings O Lemuel, it is not for kings to
drink wine nor for princes strong drink.
Lest they drink and forget the law and pervert
the judgement of any of the afflicted.
Give strong drink unto him that is ready to perish,
and wine unto those that be of heavy hearts.
Let him drink and forget his poverty and
remember his misery no more.
Proverbs 31:4-6

The Drunkard

Wine! Wine! Wine!
Bring forth more wine!
I will tell you when it is time!
Wine! Wine! Wine!
Bring forth more wine!

Be not among winebibbers.
Proverbs 23:20

The Food Chain

From the bottom of this imaginary 'food chain' it is easy to see,
All the colours of the rainbow that a man has in he.
Most are dark and dirty while a few are bright and pretty.
Humble up not humble down is usually how one travels around.
What can you do for me? What can I gain?
How will you contribute to my fortune and fame?
Will you worship and honour my great name?
Everyday is typically the same.

One can have humility that is hierarchical:
Being humble up, but not humble down.
Neal A Maxwell

The Manipulator

This poor soul bears a curse so sore,
Sometimes I wonder,
If he could possibly take much more.
He lies and He lies, He tries and He tries,

To get you to think what he wants you to,
Until one day, and it is sad to see,
That he ends up believing the lies that he told to you.
Caught in the devils web, his soul is trapped,
He needs to repent and that is that.

He that hideth hatred with lying lips, and
he that uttered a slander, is a fool.
But he that refraineth his lips is wise.
The tongue of the just is as choice silver: the
heart of the wicked is little worth.
Proverbs 10:18-20

The Drama Queen of Babylon

Today it is this!
Tomorrow it will be that!
Everyday there is always something
Going on behind your back!
Never good enough,
Always flawed,
Picks you to bits and tells everybody all.
This is how she passes the time,
She even thinks this is called having a good time.

It is as sport to a fool to do mischief.
Proverbs 10:23

The Angry

They try to put on a smiley face,
But in their mouth lies a bitter taste.
Fiercely angry, usually because of someone they had,
Who treated them badly causing them to get so mad.
Beneath the surface the flame of hate rages so intensely,
That if you were to touch them you would get burnt eventually.
So be cautious of the angry,
For they have more than often lost their sanity.
Tell them of the Gospel and its healing power,
Of the Love of Christ and of the miracle of forgiveness.
Tell them and tell them, and do this every hour.

Anger doesn't solve anything. It builds nothing,
but it can destroy everything.
Thomas S Monson

The Hypocrites

They use to go to church but not any more,
Because of the flaws in everyone that they saw.
All they see are the motes in their brethren's eyes,
While asking not: "what is this beam that is in mine?"
They will hold you to the laws
That they themselves follow no more,
And laugh and point scorn at you
From that building next door.

And why beholds thou the mote that is in thy brothers eye,
but considers not the beam that is in thine own eye?
Mathew 7:3

———⌇⌇⌇⌇⌇⌇⌇⌇⌇———

The Gossip Queen

These people are so sad and this is why you see,
They have nothing to talk about except you and me.
What's the latest? Did you hear?
But to your face its:
"How are you my dear?"

When it comes to hating, gossiping, ignoring, ridiculing, holding
grudges, or wanting to cause harm - please apply the following:
STOP IT!
Dieter F Uchtdorf

———⌇⌇⌇⌇⌇⌇⌇⌇⌇———

The Gossip Queen 2

Trust not the tongue that loves to Gossip.
For her mouth is a deep pit filled with lies.
Her words have the stench of an open sepulchre
And her mind is as cunning as a fox.
Her heart is filled with hatred and bitterness,

But concealed by deceit.
There is no method to her madness,
She is mad with unforgiveness.
Her game is to win sympathy and loyalty,
And her strategies are many.
Tears, lies, cries, laughter, aggressiveness, anger, manipulation, flattery,
And when she is confronted, ignorance.
Why! Why! I don't know why!
Both sides of the field doth she play,
Stirring everybody up in every way.
She thinks nobody is listening,
But to her surprise,
Angels are recording everything.

There is enough heartache and sorrow in this life without our adding
to it through our own stubbornness, bitterness, and resentment.
Dieter F Uchtdorf

The Sucker

He is the Gossip Queens best friend.
She gives him a reason for being.
"I will save thee O damsel in distress!"
"Your knight in shining armour! I am he!"
"I trust in your sad songs! There is no way you would lie to me!"
Sucker.

Intelligence is the Glory of God. In this
sense the sucker is far from God.

The Idiot

On par with the sucker this is he!
You will hear him asking the Gossip Queen:
"Did you lie to me?"
"No" she will say,
And he will say "oh ok".
This is the way of the idiot,
Forever will he be.
See, he is not evil,
He is just too trusting you see.
His heart may be humongous and his intentions may be well,
It's just that, well, he's an idiot.
To Heavenly Father he should turn,
That he may begin, wisdom to learn.

O Lord, I have trusted in thee, and I will trust in thee forever. I
will not put my trust in the arm of flesh; for I know that cursed
is he that putteth his trust in the arm of flesh. Yea, cursed is
he that putteth his trust in man or taketh flesh his arm.
2 Nephi 4:34

Big Heart But No Brain Syndrome

Groupies with the sucker and the idiot
These are they,
They are so trusting to those they know.
Anything they hear is absolutely true.
Their loyalty is like steel,
But their wisdom has the strength of a twig.
Here-say is valid in their court of law.
They use their brains not at all.
Opinion reigns as truth!
And reasoning to them is of little use.
Their big heart causes them not to doubt the ones they know,
But little do they know that they have big
heart, no brain syndrome too.

Cursed is he that putteth his trust in man, or taketh flesh
his arm, or shall hearken unto the precepts of men, save their
precepts shall be given by the power of the Holy Ghost.
2 Nephi 28:31

—⁓⦿⊶⊷⦿⊶⦿⊷⊶⦿⊷⁓—

The Sympathy Parties

They love to have parties where everyone gathers around,
And share their stories about how they got let down.
A passer by will smell in the air,
The dark and damp stench of despair.

And the cries in symphony can be heard:
"Did you hear how I got treated like dirt?"
Forgive and let go!
Or on your hearts this will forever hold…

Forgiveness means that problems of the past no
longer dictate our destinies, and we can focus on
the future with God's love in our hearts.
David E Sorensen

The Character Assassins

They are murderers with their mouths
The tongue is their sword.
Talk about you is what they do,
In regards to your character,
They will assassinate you.
Just like the ninja that moves in the shadows,
They will strike you with a deadly blow.
Hitting you below the belt,
Before you even know.

Folly is joy to him that is destitute of wisdom; but
a man of understanding walkers uprightly.
Proverbs 15:21

The "It's not me! It's you!"

It's not me! It's you!
Your always doing this!
And, your always doing that!
Why can't you see that it's not me! It's you!?
This poor man has no self control.
His emotions own him and he is not his own.
He takes no responsibility for how he chooses to feel.
Especially when he chooses to get angry and ill.
You made me feel like this! You made me do that!
Take some responsibility man! And that is that!
You are here to learn, how to be a master of your soul.
You are here to learn, of this, how to control.
So I suggest you take to God, your every thought.
So that he can begin teaching you,
How to hold on, to the Iron Rod.

He that is slow to anger is better than the mighty; and
he that ruleth his spirit than he that taketh a city.
Proverbs 16:32

The Self-Proclaimed VIP's

They act like they have authority from Heaven.
Capable of sentencing you to Eternal damnation.
They somehow think in their messed up heads,
That without their approval you would be better off dead!

As if they are the Saviour and Christ!
And that without their love and friendship,
Life would not be worth living.
So they think themselves grand for reaching out to you a hand,
And then look down upon you like you owe them.
This was all along their plan.
To take your friendship and then.

Have faith in yourself. One of the greatest weaknesses
in most of us is our lack of faith in ourselves.
L Tom Perry

The Addict

These poor souls, they have little control.
How to get out, they don't really know.
Deep down they want to,
They know that they need too.
But upon their souls, a fist firmly holds.
It is not gentle, it does not want to let go.
How to escape, God only knows.

Addictions are painful but the Atonement is the
cure. Pray, pray, pray and pray some more.

Storm Chasers

They love to seek out stormy weather,
By twisting your words
Or just taking everything the wrong way.
So many meanings a phrase could have,
But they would rather take it as bad.
Perhaps it is because they have never seen,
Or were never taught to think constructively.
Or grew up in an environment,
Where everyone thinks negatively.
Constructive criticism is the key,
Accompanied by honesty.
That from your errors it can set you free.
Truth is light and light is truth,
So all that is required is a new point of view.
So stop listening to satan and begin asking you know who!
For wisdom and intellect and to guide your thoughts.
For this is what he desires to do!

Stop seeking out the storms and enjoy more fully the sunlight.
Gordon B Hinkley

The Fullness of Joy

Oh these poor Babylonians, my happiness they do not know.
For they have not tasted of the tree.
Instead they continue to live in strife.

I must go through out the world,
For this message needs to be told!

Behold, my joy is full.
Alma 26:11

The Afraid

Why is he over there smiling at me?
Why is he looking so happy?
He must be having a go at me!
It is not possible for anybody to be that happy.

But Ammon said unto him: I do not boast in my own strength,
nor in my own wisdom; but behold, my joy is full, yea, my
heart is brim with joy, and I will rejoice in my God.
Ama 26:11

Hate clubs

They hear what they want to hear.
They seek out the storms.
They get into groups,
And they all hum along.

The genre of their song is hate,
About some poor person who hasn't showed up yet,
But when they do: "Hey! Come join us! Your not to late!"
These poor people are blinded to their own despair.
They can often be seen blowing into thin air.
What to do is obvious, if you cannot see,
Then here my friend lies a clue for you,
You should fall to your knees and cry to God please!
Teach me to be free! From this never ending misery!
Repentance is beautiful it will set you free,
From all that hate, that you love to breath.

Mediocrity will never do. You are capable of something better.
Gordon B Hinkley

The Marathon Runner of Light

Day by day, hour by hour,
He is receiving of Gods mighty power!
Day by day, hour by hour,
The light within, grows brighter and brighter!
Day by day, hour by hour,
More and more, does he God adore!
Day by day, hour by hour,
He will soon comprehend all!

That which is of God is light; and he that receiveth light,
and continueth in God, receiveth more light; and that light
groweth brighter and brighter until the perfect day.
D&C 50:24

The Emotionally Distorted Secret Society Supporter

How nice of them to include me!
I felt so alone, I thought I was on my own.
But now I am a part of something!
I don't fully understand what they do,
But I know for sure that it must be good!
Because they chose to, include me!
Now I am so happy!
So I will do whatever it takes!
To keep the oath and covenant that I made!
To my new friends! That love me!

Little do they know that they have been deceived.
For the sole purpose of these societies,
Is to destroy liberty.

For the Lord worketh not in secret combinations.
Ether 8:19

The Tyrannical Babylonian King

You will do this!
You will do that!
You cannot say this!
You cannot say that!
Obey me or else my temper I will loose,
And you don't want that now, do you?

Satan plans to destroy liberty - economic, political, and
religious, and to set up in place thereof the greatest, most
widespread, and most complete tyranny that has ever
oppressed men. He is working under such perfect disguise
that many do not recognise either him or his methods.
Heber J Grant

—⁓⦿⦿⦿⦿⁓—

The Godless Tyrant

Listen to me, I am right!
Do what I say, or there will be a fight!
Do what I say, and not what I do,
Because I know exactly what is good for you.
What do you know, you are just a fool.

On what basis can we morally resist tyranny? I say to you
with all the fervour of my soul that God intended men to
be free. Rebellion against tyranny is a righteous cause.
Ezra Taft Benson

The Authoritative Fool

They feel like Kings with you their slave.
This you can see by the way they behave.
A need to control the things that you do,
Even though they have no right too.
Freedom of speech what is that!
How dare you boy, question me!
Second guess me, oh you will see!
I'm going to teach you not to mess with me!

Next to the bestowal of life itself, the right to direct
that life is God's greatest gift to man.
David O Mckay

The Paranoid Militarist

World domination that is the game.
That neighbour of mine is far from tame.

He bears a smile, and comes across as friendly,
But I tapped his phone and his conversations are deadly.
He wishes us to be second to him.
It's us or them! We have to win!
Does this not justify sin?

For I the Lord cannot look upon sin with
the least degree of allowance;
Nevertheless, he that repents and does the
commandments of the Lord shall be forgiven.
D&C 1:31-32

The Imperialist

By consent or by conquest, this planet I will rule!
What's this on my chin? Oh it's drool.
I will set things straight, and make all things great!
Under my law will be all and all.
Stand with me now! Or prepare to fall.

It is the devils desire that the Lords priesthood stay asleep while
the strings of tyranny gradually and quietly entangle us until, like
Gulliver, we awake too late and find that while we could have
broken each string separately as it was put upon us, our sleepiness
permitted enough strings to bind us to make a rope that enslaves us.
Ezra Taft Benson

Eternal Grumblers

Enough is never enough
Never happy, never satisfied,
Never able to be pleased.
There is always one thing or another
These people need to go to their knees.

By and large, I have come to see that if we complain about
life, it is because we are thinking only of ourselves.
Gordon B Hinckley

The Generous Elitist

He was once poor, but now made rich!
Thanks to God! For giving him that itch!
Now he wishes his riches to share!
He travels the world looking for people who care!
Enough for others, who want to do the same!
To pass the good life on!
And Gods Holy Name!

But seek ye first the Kingdom of God and his righteousness
and all these things shall be added unto you.
3 Nephi 13:33

The Selfish Elitist

A dangerous thirst do these posses.
Quenched only by their goals of success.
But success alone is not enough,
A distinction must be made between them and us.
They would have you made a slave,
If the opportunity to them you gave.
Clever they are in their respected fields.
They seek for power and like the way it feels.
It does consume them to the bone,
They often speak down to you with an authoritative tone.

Selfishness suffocates spiritual senses.
Robert D Hales

The Partial Story Tellers

Tell the story they will, distorted and untrue,
Of how they were victimised by cruel and horrible you!
But what they did to instigate or provoke,
You will never hear not even a whisper.
As for your sympathy and loyalty they try to milk you like a goat.

Blame keeps wounds open. Only forgiveness heals.
Thomas S Monson

The Unwanted Friend

Pride,
The great and terrible destroyer of joy.
He is not yet a man but still just a boy.
Everything I do is to be better than you.
Look at me whoopee woohoo,
At how I can do everything better than you!

He that hath the spirit of contention is not of me but is of the devil.
3 Nephi 11:29

The Liar

Can you trust a liar?
If he does it to him, he will do it to you.
There is really no telling when he will make his next move.
After a while it becomes a habit,
Until eventually there is no way that he can stop it.
Whenever it's convenient or in need of a scape goat,
You best not believe anything from this mans throat.
With the Lords help through the enticings of the Spirit,
The Lord will be able to help you to overcome it.

A poor man is better than a liar.
Proverbs 19:22

Caught

When the rat is caught trying to steal the cheese,
It is easy to see how embarrassed is he.
He cries and he lies oh no not me!
Isn't it amazing how he does this with such ease.

Until we take responsibility for our actions,
improvement and progression is not possible.

The Button Pusher

Twist and turn, push and pull.
Confused and stunned you will be.
You will not know what hit you until later on,
When you reminisce and think, hang on!
He lied to me.

Not everyone is as nice as you. Or in some
cases, are they just like you?

The Predator

He is as cunning as the cat.
Waiting to pounce on the unsuspecting rat.
Still will he be, hidden behind a tree,
Waiting for the rat to near the cheese.
So he can pounce on his prey with ease.

In the premortal we knew no evil, thus deception
can come as quite a shock here, followed by disbelief
and denial at what some people are capable of.

See-Saw Hearts

I love you! I hate you!
Oh my Goodness!
What is wrong with you!

Through the promptings of the Holy Ghost, bringing to our minds
the words of the prophets that we have studied, our thoughts
and feelings can be schooled, thus preparing us to meet God.

The Yellow Belly

O man! Where is thine spine!
This world is filled with yellow-belly swine!
Love you with their lips and hate you with their hearts.
Two faced, double hearted, double crossing, back stabbing,
Cowardly, story telling, mind manipulating, swine.
Suck you with flattery and laughter.
Or with softness and kindness.
Do not be deceived!
They are as cunning as thieves.
There is little hope for these.
I'm just kidding!
There is always hope!
You just have to go to your knees!

He that goeth about as a talebearer revealer secrets: therefore
meddle not with him that flatterers with his lips.
Proverbs 20:19

The Drama Addicts

Their lives are so boring,
That any drama they find exciting.
The best kind is bad news.
To them bad news is good news.
It gives them an endorphin spike,
This they really like.

Just like a drug they cannot wait,
Until it's time to get their next hit.

A false witness shall not be unpunished, and
he that speakers lies shall perish.
Proverbs 19:9

The Blind

Of his faults he cannot see,
Heavenly Father keeps them from him a mystery.
For he does not ask to be shown,
All of the spirits that calls him home.
Therefore it be better that he not know,
All the ugly spirits that him control.
If he understood the Gospel well,
He would understand all he needs to do is yell!
Heavenly Father! Please save me from this Hell!
And one by one as he journeys toward God,
Heavenly Father will help him as he holds onto the Rod.

The Iron Rod are the commandments of God.

The Untrustworthy

Well this is going to be a short one.
This just about represents everyone!
For how can you trust a man who has not conquered all?
Still subject to the devil, that enemy of us all.
I will trust in my God above all!
Forever and ever! That I might not fall!

Thus saith the Lord, cursed be the man that
trusteth in man, and maketh flesh his arm.
Jeremiah 17:5

The Vindictive

Revenge is a dish best served cold.
These grudges in my heart I will forever hold.
You may have won the battle
But I will surely win the war!
Beware the vindictive they like to plot,
About how they can beat you and get on top.

The person a grudge will destroy the most is its bearer.

The Master Manipulator

An endless bag of tricks, he hides up his sleeve.
You will see him pull them out as he tries to deceive.
Be careful not to blink or hypnotised you will be.
Confused by the stories that he'll have you believe.
This poor soul, there is no hope for he.
I am joking of course! There is always a way!
What he should do, is be humble and pray,
And try to be better than he was yesterday.

I have seen a person carry on a charade
nearly a half decade and counting.

The Manipulator

When they are wrong they deny and deny,
Hoping you will get angry.
While they play it cool and calm,
So they can look at you like why!
Why are you getting mad!
O how dare you!
Turning the tables and shifting the blame!
This was all along their strategy and game.
These poor souls are absolutely insane.
Pray and pray, again and again!

With the help of the Holy Ghost we can find the straight and narrow.

The Stuck In It

Stuck in the deeper stages of manipulation on and on they will go,
Continuing down the same dark and dirty road.
Pretending to be who they need to be,
To maximise the efficiency of their deceit and trickery.
Like an actor in a movie they play this part well,
Often when they do this it is really hard to tell.
Because sometimes they've been doing this so long, and well,
They get stuck in it by believing their own lies as well.
These poor souls are trapped in the spider web of hell,
I pray they'll awake before it gets too late,
And to ask God to break this awful spell.

The artist of deception usually ends up deceiving himself.

The High Horse Knights

These are a self righteous bunch who like the view,
Of looking down their noses from their high horses at me and you.
Not to help or constructively criticise,
But just to demean and demoralise.

Constructive criticism to a wise man is more
precious than Gold. Take what truths these knights
carry and use it as motivation to be better.

The Mad Man

He lives in a world of terror and fear,
This man has lost everything that he once held dear.
He travels through life hoping to find,
The pieces of happiness that he had once upon a time.
But nothing can replace what he lost in his mind.
So he has gone mad by not having a clue
Oh help Me God! What do I do?
This poor man thinks he has nothing else to loose.

God can save anyone! No matter what abyss they have fallen into.

The Takers

These are a greedy bunch who like to see,
What more that they can squeeze from me!
Further do they tighten their grip on my throat,
As they strategically continue to milk me like a goat.
Whether emotionally or physically they drain,

They are in it for themselves to get gain.

The Gospel holds the light needed for salvation.

———⚬~⚬~⚬~⚬~⚬———

The Depressed Loner

Often in the shadows does he lurk.
Trying to shield himself from further hurt.
He stays by himself and thinks he enjoys his own company.
But he is sad and afraid, and very very lonely.
The pain of rejection to him are like a first degree burn.
He has taken all he cares for and desires no more.
So alone does he sit as he tries to convince,
Himself that he has all that he needs.
Heavenly Father loves you!
And can do for you what he is doing for me.

Heavenly Father and the Lord Jesus want to be your friend! Try them!

———⚬~⚬~⚬~⚬~⚬———

The Scorned

Always fearful of what to do.
Always unsure and always looking for clues.
To the hearts and thoughts of men,

And whether from heaven or hell they were sent.
Paralysed by their emotions,
And crippled by the Devils potions.
Fear and anxiety is their constant companion.
The teachings of the Gospel is their only medicine.
Their poor souls dwell in the pits of hell,
As unforgiveness and bitterness in them swells.

Salvation comes through the Atonement as
we earnestly and honestly seek it.

The Scorned 2

The desire to lift or help another,
Their fears of rejection doth completely smother.
Twisted and tied into an emotional knot,
They often turn into a complete and utter snot.
They get scared and start lashing out,
Putting others down because it temporarily helps.
To mask their feelings of insecurity.
Anyway, this is just one theory.
Perhaps if they learnt of the Fathers love,
They could forgive those by whom they were burnt.

Once you learn of the Fathers love for you, loving
those who wronged you will become easier.

The Bloke

Hurt and insecure by the strange culture here,
This poor fellow lives his life in fear.
When his friends are near he puts on a show,
Always in competition for some unknown prize,
They beat each other down often while wearing a disguise.
See inwardly they are soft and gentle souls,
But when friends are near they put on this show.
Name calling and mocking they hurt each other more!
Oh my goodness! Why do you guys do this for!
Isn't it better to lift another?
And why do you find it funny to insult each other?

We are here to help, lift, and rejoice with each other
as we try to become our very best selves.
Linda K Burton

The Con-Artist

Like a wolf he lies, in the bushes he waits.
For the right moment for him to take,
An unsuspecting little lamb,
Well this about sums up this man.

Beware, not everybody is as nice as you.

Social Exhaustion

They don't listen to understand,
They listen to reply.
Talking to them is like talking to a wall.
The spirit of anxiety has dug in his claws.
These poor people are the most miserable of all.
Judge them not for their hearts are full of sorrow.
Seek for healing from the Atonement!
Jesus will hear you, and will redeem you!

And if men come unto me I will show unto them their weakness.
I give unto men weakness that they may be humble; and my
grace is sufficient for all men that humble themselves before
me; for if they humble themselves before me, and have faith in
me, then will I make weak things become strong unto them.
Ether 12:27

The Superficial

What will they say? You can't do that!
People will talk! If you act like that!
What will they think? Oh dear me!
Hide yourself please! Don't let them see!
Oh my gosh! What will they think of me?
Don't you know how to behave?
Things like that you just can't say!
You must carry a stiff upper lip,
And when you walk, you must swing your hips.

Light is truth. Political or social correctness does
not necessarily define light and truth
Truth is truth regardless of who it pleases or displeases.
By the Power of the Holy Ghost you may
know the truthfulness of all things.
Moroni 10:5

The Dishonest Banker

Give me! Give me! Give me!
More! More! More!
Into my pockets, your money pour!
I have done the math! I know what you can afford!
I live by the saying,
The calculator is mightier than the sword!
Interest rates I will set as high as I can!
And nothing can you do,
Because the competition is my friend.

For some people, enough is never enough, thus they
linger in a never ending state of dissatisfaction.

The Politician of Babylon

I'll promise you this! I'll promise you that!
But when I'm elected, you can forget all that!
My allegiance is to those who scratched my back,
Or to he who controls the money flow.
Tell me what do those little people know?
Do you think a country they could control?
Oh what to do now with this power I hold?

We have learned by sad experience that it is the nature
and disposition of almost all men, as soon as they get a
little authority, as they suppose, they will immediately
begin to exercise unrighteous dominion.
Hence many are called, but few are chosen.
D&C 121:39-40

The Stupid

These poor people have it back the front,
They treasure up not the scriptures so they do not know,
That they are here to gather intelligence for their soul.
Instead they take pride in seeing how stupid they can be,
And then expecting you to find it funny.
There is more fun in playing it smart,
Think of all the minds you can excite with art!
Or with music reach out to touch so many Hearts!
Or think of something that you could be good at,

And how to the world you could contribute back!
What if you were good at making money!
You could feed all the hungry!
Clothe the needy and help the poor!
Wouldn't that be more fun than aspiring to being stupid and dumb?
God can help you if this you desire,
First you must be baptised and cleansed with fire,
Then Grace will he impart to make you better,
As you make his commandments your daily attire.
Their needs be an order of things,
So seek diligently, be patient and persistent,
And you will win!

The glory of God is intelligence, or, in other words, light and truth.
D&C 93:36

Whatever principle of intelligence we attain unto in
this life, it will rise with us in the resurrection.
And if a person gains more knowledge and intelligence in
this life through his diligence and obedience than another,
he will have so much the advantage in the world to come.
D&C 130:18-19

———⁓⁓⦿⦿⦿⦿⦿⁓⁓———

The Self Deluded

If I believe it then it must be true!
These poor souls confuse imagination with truth,
Overly optimistic about what they believe,
They never asked God to show them the truth.

If any man lack wisdom, let him ask of God.
James 1:5

———⁓⁓⁓⦿⦿⦿⦿⁓⁓⁓———

Conclusion

There is a way I promise you!
To find a happiness so bold and true!
A way to conquer all!
A way that you can learn how to really love!
Not only others but yourself as well!
So that you can escape this living hell!
Pray always for God to show you,
The road that leads to the straight and narrow.
On this road you will learn God's laws!
Don't just learn some but learn them all!
As you learn to apply them you will slowly feel,
An increase in love and a life so surreal!

Do you want to stay like this forever?

And if men come unto me I will show unto them their weakness.
I give unto men weakness that they may be humble; and my
grace is sufficient for all men that humble themselves before
me; for if they humble themselves before me, and have faith in
me, then will I make weak things become strong unto them.
Ether 12:27

———⁓⁓⁓⦿⦿⦿⦿⁓⁓⁓———

Treasure And Beware That Woman There

Treasure and Beware That Woman There

Treasure the woman who is humble and meek,
for of her feet you are not worthy to kiss.

Treasure the company of a woman who treasures yours,
this is how you can know if she is truly yours.

Treasure the woman whom with God seeks to polish her Soul,
time with her will never get old and in beauty she will only
grow. She seeks her Exaltation and is the wisest of all!

Treasure the woman who seeks to master the
Iron Rod, in her you will see God.

Treasure the woman who turns her every thought unto
God, and has the constant companionship of the Holy
Ghost, she will always know which way she should go,
and Heaven will be found within your home.

Treasure the woman who truly understands the word of God, for
she will never let go of the Iron Rod and together you can learn to
be one with he, so that you may both be together for Eternity.

Treasure the woman who seeks Exaltation, she is
clever for she knows she is on probation.

Treasure the woman with a beautiful Soul, you will
not regret it when you are wrinkly and old.

Treasure the woman who chooses her words carefully and

speaks from her heart, she is a rare priceless gem that from
others are set apart. She is a light that will never go dark.

Treasure the woman who is easy to read, she is
free of guile. At night you will sleep well.

Treasure the woman who is cool and calm, that easily falls asleep
in your arms, you can be sure that she will never bring you harm.

Treasure the woman who cannot lie, for you
can be sure she will not surprise.

Treasure the woman who displays loyalty, with your heart
her you can trust. For she is one of Heavens Royalty.

Treasure the woman with a modest dress,
you can be sure that she is the best!

Treasure the woman whose soul speaks safety,
this is how you can tell a real lady.

Treasure the woman open and transparent, you
can let your guard down around her.

Treasure the woman who grows her talents, you will never get bored.

Treasure the woman who loves her family, she will love you the same.

Treasure the woman who is forgiving, this you will likely be needing.

Treasure the woman who wants many children,
for she is nearly ready for Godhood.

Treasure the woman who is patient with children, she
has a good heart. She will be patient with you.

Treasure the woman who is gentle and honest, she is a
pleasure to talk to. Eternity is a very long time.

Treasure the woman who seeks to please, she is
worth crying to God for from your knees.

Treasure the woman who uses her mind, she is well worth the time.

Treasure the woman who wants to be a
wife, for she desires Eternal life.

Treasure the woman who is filled with love, for
she has been sent from Heaven above.

Treasure the woman who can stand correction, she
is capable of growth and Eternal Progression.

Treasure the woman who is playful, she will make the Eternities fun!

Treasure the woman who evil shuns, she is
a safe place to keep your heart.

Treasure a woman that is worthy to confide in, in her
bosom you may always have a safe place to hide.

Treasure the woman who stands for virtue, truth and honesty,
she is a friend of God and will likely prove herself true.

Treasure the woman who endured mortality and kept her
innocence, she is strong minded and her heart is pure.

Treasure the woman who remains cute when she is mad,
you can know that she will never leave you sad.

Treasure the woman who is free of contention,
she is among Gods finest inventions.

Treasure the woman who maketh peace, for
your house will always be at ease.

Treasure the woman who is too humble to know how high
she sits, for if she knew, that would be it for you.

Treasure the woman who can stand up tall, for
when she meets God, well will be all.

Treasure the woman with little hands, hold
onto them and never let go.

Treasure the woman whose chest are pillows,
when you tire, here you can retire.

Treasure the woman whose bosom is humble,
for they are a blessing just as special.

Treasure the woman who wants to hold your
hand, with her a life you should plan.

Love the woman with the crazy eyes, she's tired of men undressing
her with their beady eyes and falling for their crafty lies. Teach
her the Gospel, if she understands it, she will really like it.

Beware the woman who wears a bikini, she gives your
gifts away to strangers and treasures not the sacred.

Beware the woman with loose lips. Her mouth is like a cannon that
can sink ships. Not with truth, but with lies and her sweet disguise.

Beware the woman who bares a short temper, she
is not worth it. But if you have married her then
work it out, it is your fault for being stupid.

Beware the woman who is quick to anger, this should
be a warning to you that she is danger.

Beware the woman who dresses herself in shorts and singlets.
She thinketh herself a man. She is likely confused upstairs.

Beware the woman who advertises her breasts, for a rich
man can buy her with money for the right price.

Beware the promiscuous woman who giveth herself
away, least she repents and changes her ways.

Beware the woman who flaunts her body to many men, she
is likely to be a headache that will eventually go away.

Run from the woman who treasures not the Iron
Rod, she will likely lead you astray.

Beware the woman who cannot save, because of this you will pay.

Beware the woman who loves money, for
when there isn't any, will she stay.

Beware the woman with no morality, she is lost and doesn't
know the way. Anything with her will be ok. Do you
want your sons and daughters to grow up this way.

Beware the woman who despises chastity, she will with
many men play. With you she is unlikely to stay.

Beware the woman who speaks trash, her heart is likely to match.

Beware the woman who gains confidence from
flaunting her body, she is overcompensating for
insecurity, she is likely crazy or poor inwardly.

Beware the woman with a lustful heart, what will happen
when you're worn. She will wonder else where to find,
somewhere where she can get her good time.

Beware the woman who loves the ways of
the world, she will hate Heaven.

Beware the woman who is bitter and
unforgiving, to her there is no pleasing.

Beware the woman who is not easily pleased,
she will have you living on your knees.

Beware the woman who wants to pursue a career
at the expense of rearing a family here.

The Goddesses Of Zoin

Oh Father

O my Father how I pray
That you would send me a wife this day.
A wife that is loyal to me no matter what,
And has nothing but honesty in her heart!
One that won't listen to these bogeymen
As this my God scares me without end.
One that will love you more than me,
And fears you more than these silly men.
One that can see through their clever lies,
And see that they are just devils very well disguised.
One that takes the Holy Ghost,
To be her guide and her hope.
One that forgives and understands,
That I am still just an imperfect man.

You need the Spirit of God to truly appreciate the Heavenly
Beauty that a loyal daughter of God has within her.

For from the world, He keeps them a mystery.

The Jungle

I live in the Jungle, it's vegetation so lush.
With wildlife in abundance, my shoulders do brush.
There are the wolves, always on the prowl,

Looking for sheep for them to devour.
Then there are the lions and tigers who are the same,
Creeping around the long grass, playing their silly hunting game.
There are the porcupines who are prickly to touch.
And the monkeys who like to laugh hysterically and play tricks.
There are the swine who like to roll in the mud,
And the wild dogs who like to hunt in packs.
But thank God that this is not all!
For the Jungle holds creatures, most beautiful of all!
There are the doves that beautify the sky!
There are the peacocks whose feathers glorify!
There are the many patterns of the butterfly!
There are the Eagles who sore so high!
There are the horses who gallop and glide!
There are the giraffes who stand so tall!
There are the Owls who do see all!
There are the cockatiels so alert and clever!
There are the birds of every feather!
There are the elephants who always remember!
But my favourite creature in the jungle has to be the Goddess!
For without her, the Jungle would just be madness.

Who Are These Women?

Who are these women whose souls glow!
Who are these women so beautiful and bold!
Who are these women so nurturing and loving!
Who are these women so kind and caring!
Who are these women that I adore!

Who are these women who sit above all?
Who are these women who walk so tall?

———————

Perfect

Supermodels have nothing on these girls!
They are in a league of their own!
Yet to humble to admit, of just how high they sit.
Straight from Gods throne were they sent,
To show the rest of the world what God meant,
When he told us to be, even as perfect as he!

———————

A Mystery

Everywhere they go!
Follows closely a rainbow!
Visible only to those with eyes to see!
Heavenly Father from the world!
Keeps them a mystery!
The ground they walk on is paved in Gold!
The road they travel is the straight and narrow!
These Goddesses are destined to be!
One day clothed in Celestial Glory!
Where their beauty will be magnified!

In white raiment before God and Glorified!

Their Eyes!

The window to the Soul!
Through the eyes I can see!
All the hidden treasures!
That God keeps a mystery!
This did he whisper as he showed to me!
All the diamonds within them that were sparkling!
They glitter like the sun out in empty space!
And wherever they go!
Their Spirits make into a Holy Place!

Their Hearts!

Their hearts rage with a celestial flame!
That burns strong enough to make a crazy man sane!
Their Spirits are like medicine to the mind!
Able to heal the ill effects of time!
They are the riches of Eternity!
Without them, Heaven would be in poverty.
From their bowels flows a fountain of truth!
With Power to tear asunder!

All darkness with a roar of thunder!

They Are Like!

They are the fuel that keeps Eternity burning!!
They are the dreams that keep the Gods smiling!!
They are the blue that makes the sea!!
They are the rocks that hold up Eternity!!
They are the air that sustains life!!
They are every honest mans dream wife!!
They are like the canyons that make me awe!!
They are like the mountains that make me wonder!!
They are like the majesty of the crack of thunder!!
For them will be created worlds without number!!

I Wonder If They Know...

I wonder if they know.
Their hearts are able to melt the coldest soul!
Their countenance pure and white as snow!
Even in the brightest sun you can see them glow!
With a Celestial aura!
That seems to from Heaven pour!
The ambience of their surrounds intensifies!

As the beauty and colours around them seem to magnify!
Angels walk with them everywhere they go!
Guiding and protecting them.
I wonder if they know.

So Sacred

Perhaps the treasure most sacred of all!
That which I covet the most above all!
Like a priceless treasure they cannot be bought!
But only awarded directly from God!
For of the heart he is able to turn!
Just listen for the Spirit that within you will burn!
And he will show you the one to be!
The one you really want to me married to!
FOR ALL ETERNITY!!!!!!!!!!!!!!!!!

The Spice of Life

They are the Spice of Life!
Without them existence would be plain!
And the Plan of Salvation vain!
With their Celestial Colours they decorated my plate!
And upon my palate!

Still remains an after taste of Heaven!
So flavoursome and awesome!

The Closest Thing!

Now that I have found Heaven!
I can truly say!
With Power and Authority!
That this is they!
The closest thing to Heaven!
Upon this mortal sphere!
Can you not hear the Spirit!
Whisper this to your ears!

O Daddy!

O Daddy! Thank you for showing me!
So many definitions of true beauty!
Thank you for showering me!
With the hearts of your daughters!
Thank you for colouring me!
With the light of their Souls!
Thank you for igniting in me!
This fire that burns!

That I may show them!
A piece of Heaven in return!

The Devil Knows These Girls Well

If they were cast down to Hell,
This is what would happen,
I will now tell.
First the devil would roll his eyes,
Before letting out a lengthy sigh.
"Oh no! Not these girls!"
You would hear him shout and cry!
"I could not con them!"
"No matter how hard I tried!"
"Pack your bags boys we're leaving ship!"
"These girls are trouble! And just not worth it!"
Then the devils from them would flee!
While those girls, hell, would dust and clean!

So Pure

Of all the Souls that I have seen!
I have never seen any so pure!
Their hearts are like a sea of glass!

That sparkle and gleam as they walk past!
A Heavenly glow seems to shine!
From their eyes as they blink each time!
And Golden rays radiate all around them!
I think I even see a halo above them!

Hallucinating

I think I need to pinch myself!
This feels to good to be true!
I'm sure I'm asleep and in a dream!
Or hallucinating from the flu!
I must be mad! The doctors are right!
I don't know what do!

Princesses

This is their happily ever after!
This is their fairytale!
These girls are destined hereafter!
To be ordained to a life of Eternal laughter!
They are Princesses! Heirs to Gods Throne!
Temporarily departed from their Celestial home!
When they prove themselves true!

And I know that they will!
Crowned will they be!
With Heavenly Glory!
For all of Eternity!

Sweet Little Heart Melters

They are sweet little heart melters!
Can this you feel?
Like the cutest little mittens that fit just right!
Like your favourite pair of pyjamas that you really like!
Like when a parent watches their child riding his first bike!
Like the smile on a baby's face when he's asleep at night!
Like the way you feel when your sad and someone holds you tight!
Like the presence of Heavenly Father with all of his Love and Might!
Like that good feeling inside you get when you choose the right!
Like that awesome feeling when your on an aeroplane!
And it begins to take flight!

Already One

My jaw drops when this I see!
That they are already one with he!
I had to fast for 90 days!

And cry unceasingly for almost 6 years.
And even now I am not one.
But these sweet sisters of Zion,
They make me sigh in disbelief!
Oh my goodness! Oh good grief!
It's like that they were just born that way!
Already perfect! From that first day!
They get revelation and don't even know,
Because that voice they think is their own!
So finely in tune because of their gentle souls,
So meek and humble, God never lets them walk alone.
Just seeing them, reminds me of home.

Blindness

God must have blessed me with blindness to their imperfections!
For of their flaws I cannot see!
As far as I am concerned, they are perfect beings!
Such blessed creatures they are to me!
Just like them I desire to be!

Mirror! Mirror!

Mirror! Mirror! On the wall!
Who are the finest Goddesses of all?
Well that's easy King! This I say!
Look right this way!
For these are they!

To be Spiritually Minded Is Life Eternal
SMILE
2 Nephi 9:29

The Goddess Emma

The eyes are the window to the Soul,
Through hers God showed to me,
The truest meaning of Heavenly Beauty.
She chooses her words so carefully.
What she is feeling is so easy to tell,
And she is so honest and nice as well.
So cool and calm and pure in heart.
So gentle and pleasant.
Oh God can I please have her for a Christmas present?

The Goddess Leah

So young at Heart!
Innocent and pure!
Adorable and loyal!
Has the blood of a true Royal!
Another Goddess of Zion!
That Will surely endure!

The Goddess Miriam

So friendly and sweet!
With a name so brave!
This woman truly knows!
How Goddesses behave!
So playful and fun!
And evil she shuns!
This woman is enough,
To make me cry yum!

The Goddess Kenya

So gentle and sweet!
So honest and meek!
So free from contention!
She must be one of Gods finest inventions!
A peacemaker at Heart!
This spirit fills her every part!

The Goddess Anne

In her I could see, a Royal Majesty!
Who stands for Virtue! Truth! And Honesty!
Her Heart is like her dress,
Unassuming and modest.
Humbleness fills her soul,
I don't think she knows,
Not even one bit,
Of just how high she sits.

The Goddess Maddie

So sweet to talk to,
To my Heart she was medicine.
So open and transparent,
Her qualities are inherent.
Forged before she came to this mortal sphere,
She is destined to only grow,
Sweeter and dear.

The Goddess Alisha

She has a voice that can be heard from Heaven!
Capable of raising ones soul like leaven!
Angels with her sing along!
From that place where she truly belongs.

The Goddess Megan

This young woman drives four hours every week
just to see the temple!
This is how I know that she is really special.
Loves her family with all her heart

It tears her up inside to from them part.
This is how I know that she is really special.
Cares for her mother and looks out for her little sister,
This is how I know that she is really special.
Works incredibly hard to look after her family,
This is how I know that she is really special.
For her too will be created worlds without end!
For Heavenly Father sees that her works are above men.

The Goddess Tess

So tiny but yet so fierce
So much fire within her burns
Fire of passion, love and of God above
She has such smarts and a beauty within
That grows, glows and shines
Oh one day I hope that she will be mine.

The Goddess Cheri

Where has she gone? I cannot see!
The Goddess who bares so sweet a testimony.
The Spirit fills her entire being!
As the pulpit glows in Exalted Glory!

Tears roll down her cheeks as the Spirit testifies to her,
That she has so much potential blossoming inside of her.
A Goddess by nature, a daughter of God,
Who knows deep inside the truths of the rod.

The Goddess Roslyn

So soft and feminine, such a delight!
Clearly a Goddess who loves the right!
Her little body so full of might!
Filled with courage and so much light!
Clearly a Goddess who holds to the rod tight!
Oh I hope when it is time for polygamy
She and her sister don't put up a fight!

The Goddess Tamara

Never before have I seen!
One foreordained to be a Mighty Queen!
Treasures to Heart the things of God!
And has practically mastered the Iron Rod!
Has so fine a mind!
And a Soul so deep!
So humble and meek!

So beautiful and bold!
This woman has eyes!
That can pierce the Heart!
In them I saw colours!
I didn't know even existed.

The Goddess Jasmyn

So bright and cheery!!
With hopes so high!
Little does she know,
That she use to light up my sky!
Has a sneeze so cute!
It teared up my eyes.
And has a heart,
That just cannot lie!

The Goddess Celeste

Does her name not say it all?
I have never seen a woman who stands so tall,
So innocent at heart, with such child-like smarts.
So happy and free!
Just like the ocean breeze!

Truly the kind of girl,
That would send you to your knees!
Crying out dear God!
O can I have her please?

The Goddess Sophie

So cute! Even when she's mad!
Oh how dare you boy!
Cuss your mum and dad!
O how she has to be,
One of the brightest lights
That I have ever seen.

The Goddess Lindsey

Oh Lindsey your so fine!
Won't you play that violin one more time!
You dance so gracefully!
Like the deer in the wild!
I wish I had the chance to talk with you for a while.

The Woman of Light

The vibrations of her voice are soothing to the soul,
The words that she chooses are so powerful and bold.
Never doth she speak to scold,
But rather just to let you know.
She communicates well, free from manipulation,
Just listening to her brings instant relaxation.
This woman is so candid!
This woman is so splendid!

A Feminine Woman

There is nothing more desirable in this world and the next,
Than the heightened Goddess-like qualities of a feminine woman.
To be bathed everyday in the candlelight of her glow,
Oh how of this prize! I wish to know!
To drink from this elixir everyday,
Would make all of my troubles go away!
And I would feel of Heaven in every way!

I Want A Wife!

I want a wife to share with this adventure!
We would travel the seven seas!
And live out every dream!
We would live a life of meaning!
Being the answer to prayers!
We would do all the things!
That most wouldn't dare!
We would chase Gods treasures!
And one day be heirs!

I Doubly Want A Wife!

With God steering our ship! We cannot fail!
Devils may try! But to no avail!
With Wisdom from God! We will Master the Rod!
And of nothing! Will we fall short!
The wildest forests we will hike!
The greatest deserts we will cross!
The vastest oceans we will sail!
Just to stay close! To Gods tail!

Most Precious

I know a girl her name is Emma,
God is showing me of her wonder.
He says that she has never yelled
At anybody in her entire life,
That she is a woman free of strife,
And that she is the very definition
Of Heavenly Beauty!

If you want to know of your Heavenly Mother Son!
Just look at her heart!
It is bigger than the Sun!
A Goddess to be!
This is her destiny!
To be Exalted forever!
For all Eternity!
For her will be created worlds without end!
This is what for her I have planned!
An Elect daughter,
In the premortal I personally taught her,
How to be,
A Goddess and Queen!
To rule and reign
With love unfeigned!

With me Pa?
Maybe.
When you learn to be like me,
Of this beauty we shall see.
For she deserves to be treated
As a Majesty.
And you are just as rough as can be.

I'm Sorry
Please teach me some more.

———— ·ᴡᴡ∘᠊ᴄ᷍ᴇ᠋ᴛᴏ᠊ᴏᴛᴇ᠊ᴏ᠊ᴏ᠊ᴡᴡ· ————

My Dream Wife

Teach me ye Goddess of thine magnificent beauty!
Your gentleness and pleasantness equates extreme inequality!
Soaring above the Earth it reaches to the stars!
With the brightness of the sun it reveals just who you are!
Your nature is so pleasant it puts the rest of us to shame!
And with it you carry one of the Greatest of Names!

———— ·ᴡᴡ∘᠊ᴄ᷍ᴇ᠋ᴛᴏ᠊ᴏᴛᴇ᠊ᴏ᠊ᴏ᠊ᴡᴡ· ————

The Loyal Daughter of God

Her beauty is multiplied exponentially,
As she travels further along on her journey.
The nearer to God she grows,
The more her beauty glows.

A woman's beauty increases as she draws nearer to God!

———— ·ᴡᴡ∘᠊ᴄ᷍ᴇ᠋ᴛᴏ᠊ᴏᴛᴇ᠊ᴏ᠊ᴏ᠊ᴡᴡ· ————

A Best Friend

With each other! All our ambitions we will share!
To each other! We will surrender all our cares!
For each other! We would walk a thousand miles!
Toward each other! Never a frown, always a smile!
Side by side! We will conquer all our trials!
Day by day! We will find new lands in which to play!
Night after night! We will pray together for more light!
Together! To the Iron Rod we will forever hold on tight!

Together

Together we will hold God to all of his promises!
Together we will hunt for all of his treasures!
Together we will bathe in the oceans of his Love!
Together we will be humble that he will make us strong!
Together we will pray to be used in his work!
Together we will be taught to conquer all!!
Together we will awe in the majesty of his creations!
Together we will gaze upon worlds without number!
Together we will rule Kingdoms to come!
Together we will worship the Father and Son!
Together we will embrace all that is light!
Together we will work to win this fight!
Together we will seek that we may find!
All that we need to do before the end of time!

The Sweet Sister In Zion

More precious than Gold!
She seeks to do all that she has been told!
She lovingly seeks more sheep for his fold!
A loving and loyal daughter of God!
She understands the sacredness of the Iron Rod!
A Jewel of Eternity!
Exaltation is her Destiny!
An Endless posterity will be her Glory!

Anxiously Engaged

A fellow yogi she must be!
Anxiously engaged in the pursuit of spirituality!
Finely in tune with the Holy Ghost,
She can filter through the lies!
And the truth decorates her eyes!
Like the stars in the night sky!

I Pray

Of her goodness I pray for my heart to be branded!
And that we may always have each other and never left stranded!
That we may seek God with all of our strength!
That he may clothe us with his unconditional Love!
And that the Angels be not restrained!
And guide us to that which we aim!
And that they may rain upon us the Celestial Fruits!
And every other blessing of Heaven!

The Goddess Beside The Window Sill

She rests beside the window to Heaven
Gazing inside with her eyes!
She seeks after the treasures of Eternity
And works diligently to win the prize!
Her heart is honest and her mind so pure!
That without a sweat, she so easily endures!
The Spirit teaches to her the Heart of God!
As she anxiously strives to hold tighter to the Iron Rod!

A Wife

O Father! What is a wife?
Ah my son this is she!
She is the bringer of life!
The giver of Joy!
She is the friend in whom you may confide!
She is the one with whom you will share this ride!
She is the one whom will be by your side!
Through all the lows and all the highs!
Side by side if you come before me,
I will make Great and Exalt thee!
That forever and ever together you may learn!
All of the treasures of Eternity!
Do not underestimate the preciousness of a wife!
For without her, there can be no real life!
Are you ready son? Can you see?
This is life's greatest mystery!
Thank you pa!

What Is A Family?

Oh Father! What is a Family?
Ah my Son! This is they!
Those available always to play!
Those who will say to you!
Never go away!
They are those whom will hold you close!

They are those who will always have time!
They are those whom you will call mine!
They are those to whom you will be sealed!
They are those with whom you will before me kneel!
They are those with whom you will pray!
They are those whom you will teach everyday!
They are those whom you will nurture and love!
They are those whom I will send to you from above!
Thanks Pa!

Tireless

Nothing is more attractive to a King!
Than a woman who loves to learn!
Treasures to Heart the things of God!
And prays unceasingly for the Spirit to burn!
Seeks tirelessly to be prepared to be one with God!
As she prays for the Spirit to teach to her the ways of the Iron Rod!
Everyday she tries again hoping to hear him say!
This is the way my precious child!
You'll never leave home again!

None Can Compare

Of their beauty none can compare!
The Goddesses of Zion!
My I wouldn't dare!
They are all out of my league!
They are from a place so high!
Whenever they walk by,
All I can mumble is Hi.
Their Celestial rays keep me in a daze!
With my jaw dropped open,
I am kept in this stupid haze.

Please Give Me One To Love

Oh Great God from on high!
Won't you please hear my cry!
I am so lonely, of this it pains me.
Won't you give me a Goddess
To love and caress!
To wed and to bless!
To live and worry less!
To celebrate with all the joys of Heaven!
To make it together to the Celestial Kingdom!
Oh Great God from on high!
Please give me one to love!

So Mysterious

They are so gentle!
They are so sweet!
Roses are red!
And so are their cheeks!
How is it that they
Are so humble and meek!
The Spirit doth whisper:
"They are elect!"
Oh my! Oh my!
No wonder! No wonder!
That every time I see them!
I hear the Earth roar its thunder!

When Will I A Goddess Win

They are so terrible!
They are such a tease!
To be so beautiful!
It should be a sin!
Oh Great God!
When will I a Goddess win?
I can take no more!
My Heart is anxious!

To know what it will be like!
To have a Goddess to be blessed with!

Rich

Their wealth is spiritual!
Their holiness ritual!
God fearing by nature!
God loving by nurture!
The type that would never hurt you!
The type that just wants to be with you!
I wish I could stop lying!
For of all this my heart I am denying.
Father says one he is preparing!
So here I am just patiently waiting!

Dreaming

The Gospel of the Gods they love to learn!
Their beauty within them causes my Heart to burn!
Some have a glow I have never seen!
As if God is in them and outwardly he beams!
Father do you hear my cries?
Who is the one that will be my prize?

Be patient Son your nearly there!
Soon your dreams will be taken care!
She is nearly ready and so are you!
So just keep following me and you know who!
Yay!
Thanks Papa!

What Is Love

Father what is love?
It is an appreciation!
A deep concern for another's well being!
It is what makes a Heart sing!
A feeling of warmth!
A fountain of light!
A strength from within!
A pleasing delight!
A pleasure well worth your fight!
Don't worry Son I will teach you!
And your wives!
Goodnight!
Goodnight Pa!

Talking With Jesus

What do you want to do Nick?
Shall we save the world?
Let's start with something simpler,
Like finding you a girl!
It's not so simple Lord,
I want a real Lady!
One that's nice to talk to,
And won't drive me crazy!
One who doesn't wear singlets
And thinks she's a man!
One who likes to wear dresses
And knows fully, your plan!
One who wants to marry!
And have lots of kids!
One who's a little cheeky
And full of wit!
One who's smart
And really stands apart!
Perhaps, she may
Even be good at art?
Find me her Lord
And then we'll talk,
About saving the world
Cause I'll put it in short.
I need a girl.

True Beauty

A woman with a beautiful soul
Is the treasure of a King!
For with wealth untold
Anything he can have.
But a woman with a beautiful soul,
Cannot be bought, not even with Gold!
She needs no guise, yet in her mind, she is wise!
For she follows in the paths of righteousness!
And blessed is she for her holiness!
Pleasant is her nature and gentle are her ways,!
And hypnotising, is her gaze!
And intelligence she possesses, that simply amazes!
Worthy to receive from her King, endless praises!
A beauty unknown, a masterpiece of God!
Who holds firm, to the Iron Rod!
Studies hard the things of Eternity!
And embraces well, her Divine identity!
Oh how I wish to share, with her my Destiny!

———⟊⟊∘⟊⟊∘⟊⟊∘⟊⟊∘⟊⟊∘⟊⟊———

The Song Of Love Continues

Nothing is more attractive to a King,
Than a heart, that he has to win!
And effort she requires him to put in!
If he wishes her heart, to one day win!
For that which cometh easy,

Often blows away with the wind!
And a house will not stand,
If it is built upon sin!
Forged in the crucible of God!
And refined in his fire!
His principles, must be her daily attire!
Her countenance pure and without flaw!
For to God, her heart, doth she constantly pour!
Her mind clear and never misty!
And her face, so very pretty!
With her money, she is thrifty!
And with her heart, she is picky!
Dear Great God, finding her will be tricky!
So I am thankful, that I have you.

Where Is She?

I want to marry a Queen!
I want to marry a Goddess!
I want to marry
A Later Day Princess!
Oh Great God!
Would you find me the One!
The one that would be, oh so much fun!
And we could together,
Raise children forever!
According to the pattern
Set by the Gods in Heaven!
Forever and ever

We would dwell!
In thy presence
And thy Glory!
Forever and ever
We will reign!
And rule with Love!
A Love unfeigned!
Oh dear God
Where is she?
Oh dear God
Would you send her to me?
Oh dear God
How happy would I be!

———⁓⁓◦◦⁓◦⁓◦⁓◦◦⁓⁓———

The Spine Of Eternity

Oh how treasure some are the joys of family,
They are the spine of Eternity!
Upon them doth all else rest!
Kingdoms! Dominions! Glories! And all the best!
Oh how the thought doth make me tear,
To know that forever I might rear!
A posterity so numerous,
That like the Stars in the sky,
Will continue forever, and never ever die!
Oh how I feel like Abraham of old,
Who wept with joy when to him God told!
To look at the stars and to try to count them!

For numberless shall they be!
And I shall bless them!

How Boring

How boring would Eternity be,
If I had not a family, for me to accompany?
I would be by my lonesome,
Destined forever to dwell,
By myself, in a living hell.
Nobody to play with,
Nobody to tell,
Nobody to share,
All the treasures there.
How boring would Eternity be,
If I had not a family,
To accompany me?

The Solution

A large family I must have!
So that we never get bored!
Enough to fill an orchestra!
Enough to perform a play!

Enough to fill a choir!
So I can listen to them sing all day!
Oh Great God won't you bless me!
With an incredibly large family,
Because how boring would Eternity be,
Without an incredibly large family?

———❦———

Your Loyal Daughters

Your loyal daughters my God
They are so beautiful!
The ones that to you follow true!
Their countenances shine
Like I have never before seen!
Oh how this to me
Must be Heavens Greatest Mystery!
They are so precious with their innocent stares,
They are so Holy I wish to join with them as heirs.
They are the Jewels of Eternity!
Heaven wouldn't be Heaven without them,
Why you love them so dearly
I can clearly understand.
Thank you for allowing me to see
Just for a moment their truest beauty,
Which coupled with Glory from on high
Will a hundred fold magnify.
They are so gentle just like the breeze
I can see myself falling in love with them with ease.
Oh how they bring me to my knees

Crying out to God Please!
Please make me worthy
And someone who deserves,
To spend Eternity, with all of these Girls!
Make me something Great!
That they can look up to!
Someone to be admired
By they who are so beautiful!
My life I place in your hands Jesus
For this I know,
That you truly understand.

To My Number One Wife!

I want so many children!
One wife won't do!
I want them by the thousands!
That would be too much for just you!
So tell your relatives and friends
To come join our family!
Together we will live!
Eternally happily!
With all of our kids!
One humongous family!
Planets will we fill
Throughout the ages!
Govern them we will
With Love and Kindness!
To us they will address

"Your Royal Highness!"
Our Royal family!
They will Eternally be
Our Everlasting Glory!

Apparently

Apparently to qualify
For Eternal Life,
God commands that
I have more then one wife!
It's true!
If you don't believe me,
See D&C 132
Read it carefully
He leaves you a clue!
He starts to explain it
In verse one and two!
So I kneel down in prayer
And ask God
What do I do?
Because when I tell the girls this
They look at me like
Oh shame on you!

When I Have A Wife!

When I have a wife!
I will give to her my life!
I will love her so dearly!
And never forsake!
I will take her by the hand
To the pearly white gates!
It will be so much fun!
To finally have someone!
With whom I could,
This race run!
We will help each other up
When the other falls down,
With a loving smile and never a frown.
We will show each other what love is!
And then we will teach it to all of our kids!
With our love we would be so rich!
With the Eternal prize glittering in our eyes!
We will master all the teachings to Eternal life!
To each other we will hold on tight!
As our battles we will together fight!
Praying to our God to help us to stay,
To the Iron Rod and to lead us all the way!

Kindness

If you were standing at the gates
To the celestial kingdom,
Those which lead to the highest degree.
And you saw one mourning
In misery and agony.
Because she had not a priesthood holder
For her to accompany,
Her to the kingdom
Of God and his Glory.
Would you not offer her
To come and join your family?
So that she may enter
Into the highest degree?
To partake of the blessings
Which await in eternity?

To be a righteous woman during the winding up scenes on this earth, before the second coming of our Savior, is an especially noble calling. She has been placed here to help to enrich, to protect, and to guard the home--which is society's basic and most noble institution.
Spencer W. Kimball

The Songs
Of Nick

―――∽∾⚮∾∽――――

Rewards

Let the pauper eat, drink and be merry.
Let the wise man seek wisdom and God's Glory.
Let truth and knowledge be the treasure of Kings,
That the hearts of their people they may win.
Let exaltation be the prize for he,
Who works diligently to conquer sin.
That he may seek his reward expectantly,
And that it will not be taken from him.

Remember, your goal is Exaltation and Eternal Life!
Russell M Nelson

Who Are You?

Heavenly Father, who are you?
Ah my son, this is I!
First and foremost I am your Father!
And to you, there will be none above me ever!
But besides that I like to learn!
All the knowledge that my Father has learned!
He teaches to me as I teach to you!
This is the Gospel that you know to be true!
You are still young, the basics come first!
Psychology and Philosophy the ways to life!
And the most important is coming!
How to love your wives!

Thank you Heavenly Father for loving me.

In this Church the man neither walks ahead of his
wife nor behind his wife but at her side.
Gordon B Hinckley

———⁓⁓◦◦○◦⊙◦⁓◦⁓———

Tell Them Dad

Heavenly Father,
People on this Earth think that you are a 'yes man',
I tell them they are wrong but they think me dumb.
Can you tell them who you are please.
I am the Lord! God of Gods! Kings of Kings!
And Father of Fathers!
I hold true to the Iron Rod!
The Law that binds us in the Eternities!
I am the Judge of Mercy and Justice!
That if you repent you will feel!
I am the Father of your Spirits!
Always willing to teach you to develop it!
Come unto me and I will teach you peace!
That if you learn you will be free!
I will make thee Gods if thou will obey!
Partake of my ordinances and pray pray pray!
Turn unto me your every thought!
Throughout the day, everyday!
That I might lead you, guide you and direct you!
And show to you the way!
But if you don't!

In the Eternities you will regret this everyday.
Thanks Pa!

In the Eternal worlds there are but Gods and servants (angels) and servants of servants. The Sacred Power of procreation is held only by Gods. The Masters of the Gospel. That they may teach it to their Spirit children brought forth from a place beyond, giving them an opportunity for development and potentially Godhood too! They will be Gods! Fathers! And Kings! To their Children Forever and Ever!

"Now, it may be contended that a judgment, with some degree of salvation for all, encourages the sinner to pursue his dark ways. Not so. However generous the judgment, it is measured by our works. Our punishment will be the heavy regret that we might have received a greater reward, a higher kingdom, had our lives conformed more nearly to truth. Such remorse may yield keener pain than physical torture." (Understandable Religion, p. 89)
John Widtsoe

What is a Wife?

O Father! What is a wife?
Ah my son this is she!
She is the bringer of life!
The giver of Joy!
She is the friend in whom you may confide!
She is the one with whom you will share this ride!
She is the one whom will be by your side!
Through all the lows and all the highs!

What Manner Of Man Is Thee?

What manner of Man is thee?
That the world's most beautiful girls
Sing praises, worship and love to you,
What manner of Man is thee?
That Kings and Queens kneel at thy feet,
What manner of Man is thee?
That everyday thou helpest me,
What manner of Man is thee?
That when mountains see you they do flee,
What manner of Man is thee?
That can even calm the Mighty Sea,
What manner of Man is thee?
That with two fingers thy lit the sun,
What manner of Man is thee?
That when Devils hear you they do run,
What manner of Man is thee?
That Heavenly Father even calls you Son.

He is our captain, the King of Glory, even the Son of God!
Thomas S. Monson

———∿∽᎐᎐᎑᎐∿———

Only The Beginning

The principles of the Gospel is the recipe for Liberty.
By obedience to it, Man, Woman and Child can live truly free.
Through all the generations, through all the ages.

From Eternity to Eternity, everybody gets their chance.
To experience in mortality the Gospel of totality.
To embrace it absolutely, or reject it completely.
It incorporates all truths, that have been trialled and proven true,
But children being children, must start with just a few.
Humility, humble and stripped of pride,
Honesty, virtue and full of love inside.
Compassion and mercy, and being absolutely forgiving,
If we can but master these, there will be more coming.
The road of progression will go on for those,
Who mastered the basics by listening to the Holy Ghost.
Line upon line, precept upon precept,
Closer and closer, their countenance grows.
And when they become just like him,
The knowledge that awaits them,
God only knows.

There is no other one item that will so much astound
you, when your eyes are opened in Eternity, as to
think that you were so stupid in the body.
Brigham Young

⸻ ∿◦♋◯✦✿◦∿ ⸻

The Masters

A totality of freedom for all can be found,
In the Gospel of Jesus that was to him passed down.
By the generations before him from Father to Son,
Now it is our turn to accept it or to forever shun.
The Gospel portrays a way of life,

That all can live in peace and free from strife.
Free from contention in peace and harmony,
It teaches us the way to absolute Liberty.
Liberty does not mean do as you will,
For to whose Liberty would you then steal?
Instead it involves laws and personal development,
To the point where all that exists is love and compassion.
Say me crazy and that it cannot exist,
But this my friends is how the Gods live.
For they are Masters of the Gospel,
Having mastered it while they were mortal.
They took the Holy Ghost to be their guide,
The succour of their Saviour they cherished inside.
And when the day came at the end of their mortal life,
They were ordained God's to forever preside,
Over the generations that from them would flow,
They will teach and nurture their children
that from them would grow,
Giving them the opportunity for this Gospel to know.
From Eternity to now this has gone on,
And from now to Eternity it will forever go on.

How many Gods there are, I do not know. But there never
was a time when there were not Gods and worlds, and when
men were not passing through the same ordeals (mortality)
that we are now passing through. That course has been
from all Eternity, and it is and will be to all Eternity.
Brigham Young

The Gospel of Jesus Christ

How simple is the Gospel,
Yet so complex.
Harder to master
Than the most advanced math!
It's teachings are plain,
It's truths are simple.
Yet how I struggle,
To master it's principles.
Through error do I learn
As I feel and see!
All the dead ends
Does he show to me!
As long as I persist,
I will win!
For he has died,
For the forgiveness of my sins.
The way is straight,
The path is narrow.
Brothers and sisters
This is the road to follow.
The greatest reward
Lies at the end,
Of this road travelled
By the greatest of men.
I can tell you now
Where they dwell,
But the Grandness of their Glories
Can only be beheld!

This Gospel is so simple a child can grasp it, yet so
profound and complex that it will take a life time - even an
Eternity - of study and discovery to fully understand it.

Dieter F. Uchtdorf

———— ∽∽◦✦◦✦◦∼∽ ————

The Gospel Is Restored!

Brothers and sisters!
Friends and foe!
I wish to tell you
Of matters you need to know!
We are here for a reason!
A reason unknown,
Until God restored the prophets!
Again! The same as of old!
They walk the Earth again
Just as in days of old!
They carry the same message
That Jesus told!
With authority from God,
The Priesthood they hold!
To perform the sacred ordinances
That you need to return home!
There's baptism by water,
For the remission of sins!
And baptism by fire
To cleanse you from within!
This is the Gift of the Holy Ghost
By the laying on of hands.
Once you receive it
You will never be the same again!
If you keep the commandments

And strive to be like Jesus,
Taking guidance from the spirit
Through its quiet whispers.
Feel and see
The things to do,
And try to stay
On the straight and narrow.
Which will one day lead you
To the place you'll want to be,
At the end of your probation
In this torturous mortality!

"It's true isn't it? Then what else really matters?"
Gordon B Hinckley

Isn't It Obvious?

Here here! Listen closely!
Lend me your ears and listen carefully!
I have something to say!
I have something to tell!
So here, here! And lend me your ear!
The spirit of God speaks again to man!
This is all part of Heavenly Fathers plan!
First you must be baptised into his church!
The one that bears, the name of his heir!
The Church of Jesus Christ of Later Day Saints
Isn't it obvious?

So many churches! They all teach slightly
different things! Which one is true?
Isn't it Obvious!

The Wealth Of The Gods

The Mastery of Emotion is the wealth of the Gods!
The more one grows! The richer he becomes!
Dominion over self is highly rewarding!
The Fruits of this tree are extremely empowering!
Just one bite and you will be hooked!
More! And More! You will want!
To God you must cry!
O help me please!
I beg thee God from my knees!
Please make me Great!
Even as thee!
Rely on my wisdom and I will teach thee!
For I cannot help you unless you listen.
So turn unto me your every thought!
And I will whisper that which you sought!

Your mission is preparation. It is your school to Eternity!
Spencer W Kimball

Congratulations On Your Baptism

Congratulations on your baptism
You have opened the front door.
Now it's time to wonder in
And to take the time to explore.
All that this castle has to offer,
All that it has in store!
Such treasures lie within,
As you explore the many corridors.
Eternal treasures to win,
And there is always more.
You will discover
As you turn to the Holy Ghost.
The Spirit sent by God
To be your host.
Fountains of living water
That will never run dry.
Such treasures lie in storage
That will make your heart cry.
Tears of joy
That will make you wonder why.
Why anyone would do
The things that God does.
The answer to your question friend,
Is because he loves us.

The Gospel is a fountain of knowledge that never runs dry.
Gerald Causse

Heavens Worth

To chase for Gold and Silver
Oh what a chore,
How this for me
Has become but a bore,
For I have found much greater,
Knocking on Heavens door.
Such treasures have I found,
Such wonders so profound,
Such mysteries I can feel,
I will search for them with zeal,
I will muster all my might
To forever choose the right,
For I now know
That Heavenly Father is always right!

I know the scriptures and I understand them.
Joseph Smith

Begin To See!

O the world! What a bore!
Now I can see! So much more!
Compared to Eternity!
This world it seems!
Is a black and white!
Colourless dream!

And yet it is filled!
With so much wonder!
Beauty and majesty!
And so much colour!
So I hope that through these words!
You can begin to see!
Into the Realm!
That is Eternity!

Just think of it!
You are known and remembered by the most majestic,
powerful and glorious being in the universe! You are loved
by the King of infinite space and everlasting time!
Dieter F Uchtdorf

Heaven's Treasures

What deeper meaning there is
To be found in the scriptures!
They are like a vault
Of never ending riches!
Deeper and deeper do they grow!
Until they are written upon your Soul!
Come and feast
Upon this feed,
And the treasures you will find
Will be just what you need.
More valuable than any
Earthly rare,

For Gold and Silver
Cannot even compare!
I guarantee you treasures
That will make you stare,
Up into Heaven
You will cast your glare.
In awe and wonder
As you pray,
And as you ponder.

"Ponderize"
80% extended pondering
20 % memorisation
Create a higher place for your thoughts to go.
What verse will you ponderize this week?
Devin G Durrant

My Favourite Story

How wonderful it is to ponder
About heavens mysteries!
They shake me like asunder
As I awe and I wonder!
One day I will grasp
All that heaven asks!
And he will unfold to me!
All, at last!
What more could I ask for?
What more could I want?

What else is there?
What else compares?
To be like the father
Is all that I care.
All the Earthly treasures
Have simply lost their flare.
They mean nothing to me
No, not anymore!
For seeking the Grandness of God's Glory
Has become my favourite story!

Mans chief concern in life should not be the acquiring of gold, or of
fame, or of material possessions. It should not be the development
of physical prowess, nor of intellectual strength, but his aim, the
highest in life, should be the development of a Christ-like character.
David O. Mackay

—⁓⸝⸎⸏⁓⸎⸏⸎⸎⸝⸎⸎⸝⸎⁓—

The Generations

All currently in mortality
Are but one generation,
Children of God's who live in the third kingdom.
(2 Corinthians 12:2 KJV)
They too also are children of children,
Fathers of Fathers and Mothers of Mothers.
If and when your mind can expand,
In regards to this matter to comprehend,
You will see, just how tiny,
That we are compared,

To Eternity.

As there be Gods many, and Lords many.
1 Corinthians 8:5

The Universe We Live In!

Policed by righteousness
Do they sit,
Upon their thrones
They are filled with wit.
The Holy Priesthood
They do bear,
Sitting Exalted
Upon their chair.
Serving under
The Holy One!
The Loving one
Who sent his Son!
Angels serve them
And do their will,
Teaching their children
To fit the bill.
To be Gods
Just like they,
So they can find joy
In their Glorious ways!
But not all follow
In their footsteps,

Instead other ways
Do they tread.
How this gives them
Reason to mourn,
To see their children
Become torn.
By living lives
Filled with sin,
The Eternal prize
They will not win.

The Priesthood of God, that was given to the ancients and is given to men in the latter days, is co-equal in duration with eternity—is without beginning of days or end of life. It is unchangeable in its system of government and its Gospel of salvation. It gives to Gods and angels their supremacy and power, and offers wealth, influence, posterity, exaltations, power, glory, kingdoms and thrones, ceaseless in their duration, to all who will accept them on the terms upon which they are offered.
Brigham Young

My Heavenly Family

As the fog begins to clear,
Such wonders I can see.
All those things,
That were once a mystery.
Such as the Love
That my Heavenly Family has for me.

Angels do protect me
Each and every day.
Brother does teach me
To walk in his ways.
And Father sends his spirit
To gently light the way.
As for Mother
I just know that she is there.
Because I can always feel
Her tender Love and Care.

Families are the treasure of Heaven.
Neil L Anderson

God's Love

The Greatest of God's mysteries
Has to be his love,
Oh such a mystery
Poured down from above.
So unconditional
It is hard to conceive,
So forgiving
I can hardly believe.
When I feel it
It makes me weep,
One day when i see him
I will fall at his feet,
And tell him that I love him

When we finally meet.

The atonement is the greatest evidence we have
of the Fathers love for his children.
Linda K Burton

He Will Hear Your Prayer

Come and learn the ways of love,
Through the instructions
Sent from above.
They teach us to live
Freely and in peace,
Free from contention
The cause of all destruction.
So come one, come all
And learn how not to fall,
You will stumble
You will stutter,
Perhaps sometimes
You will even utter,
I don't understand
What this is about?
Oh won't you God
Please help me out!
Just kneel down
And say a prayer,
He will hear
Of this I declare!

You will hear
A still small voice whisper softly:

Oh dear child,
Do you know,
Just how special
You really are?
Or how you hold
Such potential,
Even of things
Still untold.

The gospel of Jesus Christ can transform life from the
ordinary and dreary to the extraordinary and sublime.
Dieter F Uchtdorf

His Love

When my eyes start to water
And my bosom starts to burn,
Oh for that feeling
Do I long and yearn,
How I want to tell you
Exactly how it feels,
But words cannot describe
This love that feels so real,
If only I were able to
If only I could,

Describe it to you somehow,
You know I would,
But hey don't be sad
Cheer up! And be glad!
For he says to tell you
That he really loves you!
And that he is waiting
To hug and kiss you,
That he is there
When your ready
To come to him...
He's holding the door open,
You just have to come in...

If you get lost...
Or don't know the way...
Ask him for directions
And he will light the way!
Guide you and direct you
Through the Holy Ghost,
Remember that he loves you
Each and every day,
And if you want to find him
All you have to do is pray...

He loves us because He is filled with an infinite measure of holy, pure, and indescribable love. We are important to God not because of our résumé but because we are His children. He loves every one of us, even those who are flawed, rejected, awkward, sorrowful, or broken. God's love is so great that He loves even the proud, the selfish, the arrogant, and the wicked.
Dieter F Uchtdorf

Whatever sin or weakness or pain or struggle or trial

you are going through, he knows and understands
those very moments. He loves you.
Linda S Reeves

I will persist! I will pursue!

Nothing can stop me!
Not no one!
From keeping me from seeing,
The Holy One!
I will persist!
And I will pursue!
Following the trail
Of endless clues!
Left to me by Jesus
Through his chosen ones.
Prophets and Apostles,
The appointed ones.
Listen to them carefully
And learn of their words,
They speak words of wisdom
And of the ways of him.
Which if you listen
Will teach you
To conquer sin.
So that come that day
He will let you in,
Because no unclean thing
Can enter in.

Sometimes courage is the little voice at the end of
the day that says, "I'll try again tomorrow!"
Thomas S Monson

It will all be worth it!

Oh how this very Gospel
Has stolen all my heart,
After the cruel world,
Tore it all apart,
But with all the teachings,
That Jesus did impart,
To me through his spirit,
And Prophets whom he set apart,
Oh what Power, I once never knew,
Could reverse the wounds, caused by a thoughtless few.

Forgiveness and repentance, just try a little bit,
And my grace I will impart upon you
To humble and renew.
You will grow and you will learn,
How to be like me!
So come little one,
And join me in my never ending glory!
Forever will we reign
In Exalted Spheres on high
No more suffering
No more pain,
Come, dry your eyes.

Cry no more little one,
Here, let me cast away your pain.
Rejoice with me now,
For it was not all in vain!
Look how strong you are!
Unbreakable like steel!
Rejoice with me now!
For all of this is real!
You have conquered all there is!
And overcome the world!
Come with me friend!
Together we will live!
Forever together!
One big, happy, family!

Revelations 2:26

It is often during the difficult times that we learn
the most, as painful as the lessons may be.
Thomas S. Monson

———— ‿ᴖ‿ᴖᴏᴄᴇᴏᴏᴖᴇᴏᴏᴖᴖ ————

The Tree of Life Which
is the Love of God

Oh how Great
The Greatest of all,
The most sacred treasure, of them all,
It's depths are boundless
It reaches deep,

Into your Soul,
It will make you weep,
It feels so warm,
Makes you happy you were born,
Keeps you calm
Even in the worst of storms.
I speak of the mightiest gift of all,
The most desired, above them all.
Do you feel it everyday?
If not, Tis to your dismay,
On your knees should you fall,
And pray to the God, who is above all,
To teach you to be worthy of this gift
That is the most desired, of them all.
And if you feel it everyday,
To Ye whom posses it, I can only say,
To falter not, and not to stray,
For it groweth, more and more,
Each, and every day.

I marvel to think that the Son of God would condescend to save us,
as imperfect, impure, mistake-prone, and ungrateful as we often are. I
have tried to understand the Savior's Atonement with my finite mind,
and the only explanation I can come up with is this: God loves us
deeply, perfectly, and everlastingly. I cannot even begin to estimate
"the breadth, and length, and depth, and height of the love of Christ."
Dieter F Uchtdorf

God's Gifts

It is Christmas everyday
When your friends with the Lord,
As a new gift everyday
He desires to send your way.

Do you wish more love little one?
Do you want some more?
Tell me what can I give you?
What can I pour?
How about some talents to impress the girls?
Here, have these here.
What else can I do for you?
What else do you need?
Wait! Why am I asking you?
I am God! I know exactly what you need!
Here little one, be patient and obey.
Do everything that I say
And I promise that one day.
You will be Great and Mighty!
Just like me and Father.
The Greatest of Greats
The Highest Of Highs!
We live in a place,
Where even angels cannot fly!

If we earnestly appeal to God, he takes us as we are
and makes us more than we ever imagined.
Neill F. Marriott

Oh Eternity

I wish that I could see what awaits me in Eternity!
How joyous I would be! How joyous would be me!
What treasure do await! When I enter that Gate?
I wish I could see through the Portals of Immortality!
How joyous I would be! How joyous would be me!

Nature is the glass reflecting God, as by the sea reflected
is the sun, too glorious to be gazed on in his sphere.
Brigham Young

———◦◦◦◦◦◦———

Oh Eternity, Eternity

Oh Eternity
Oh Eternity
Thou art a mystery,
How long art thou Eternity
Oh Eternity, Eternity,
If only I could see
What it meant to be
Living in Eternity, oh Eternity,
Then maybe I would try
A little harder here,
In the confinements of
This humble mortal sphere
To do all that is required of me
So that some day I may be,

Able to abide with my Father in all of his Glory,
Exalted in the Highest,
For all Eternity...

What of thou,
Oh wondrous Eternity,
Why not unfold,
Your mysteries to me?
Why keep me in the dark?
Oh Eternity.
But wait I see a spark,
Oh could this be?
A glimpse through the veil, into Eternity!
Oh thank you for showing me!
What is to be!
What is awaiting for me!
In Eternity!

Man's earthly existence is but a test as to whether he will concentrate his efforts, his mind, his soul upon things which contribute to the comfort and gratification of his physical nature, or whether he will make as his life's pursuit the acquisition of spiritual qualities.
David O McKay

———— ∿⚬⚬⚬⚬⚬∿ ————

I Am The Way

Through the gift of repentance,
And also the power of Grace,
Man can be redeemed,

To live again in that Holy place!
All you have to do is follow the shepherd,
The one who invited all to come follow me.
I am the way, the truth, the light,
I am the road to everlasting life.
Come and learn my teachings child,
And in your heart you will know they are right.
Study my words every night,
And try to apply them throughout the day,
By listening to the spirit,
Whisper to you as you pray.

Whatever the cost of repentance, it is swallowed
up in the joy of forgiveness.
D Todd Christofferson

—⁓⦚⦚⁓—

Please...

If the heavens were to open
At this very moment,
Would I stammer, would I stumble
Would I quake, would I tremble,
Would I fumble, would I mumble,
Oh Father would I grumble?
Please don't leave me here
I want to come,
Please don't leave me here
Father I'm done,
I don't want to live here

After what I've seen,
Please don't leave me here
Father I'll be clean,
I will do all that you ask
Just to get a pass,
Please don't leave me here,
Please.

If we knew that we would meet the Lord
tomorrow... What would we do today?
Dallin H Oaks

———— ·∾◦⌒◦⌒◦∿· ————

The Dare

Such treasures do await,
Guarded,
by the keeper of the Gate,
Hurry friends hurry
For the day doth grow late,
You have only a short time
To listen to this rhyme
So hurry friends hurry,
Do not
fall behind.

Come and develop,
Your whole Soul he will envelop,
Teach you to be
Just like he,

So that you may escape
That endless misery.
Come and learn the ways
Of life eternal,
For how joyful its rays
Oh how supernal!

Nothing can compare
So I issue you this dare,
To become like him
Only because I care.

Mans chief concern in life should not be the acquiring of gold, or of
fame, or of material possessions. It should not be the development
of physical prowess, nor of intellectual strength, but his aim, the
highest in life, should be the development of a Christ-like character.
David O. Mackay

—~~o~e~o~e~o~~—

Can Ye Think Of Greater?

What could be more precious,
Than to recognise the promptings of the spirit?
To know that which your Father
Desires to tell you.
What could be more precious
Than to be,
A constant companion to he?
He who wishes,

To be your teacher and friend.
He who was once but a man.
Now not just a God.
But the highest of all.
He who reigns
Exalted above all.
Desires to help poor and simple you.
To do great deeds,
That if left to you.
Would have great need,
In order to do.
So listen carefully and pay close attention.
Because this my friends,
Is of the utmost importance.
For if you wish to dwell with him,
Do you not think you should listen in?

Pray to Heavenly Father, listen to the Holy Ghost, follow the
promptings you are given, and all will be well in your life.
Robert D Hales

When Did The Gods Begin To Be?

Passed down from generation to generation
Through all Eternity,
Does any man know when the Gods began to be?
Or how they gained the knowledge
Of all things true?

And learnt how to use it
To help me and you?
How did they master
The ways of love and peace?
When did their civilisations begin to peak?
When did Godhood did they reach?
All these questions do blow my mind!
But I know that I will find out in due time.

Give me patience to wait until I can understand for myself.
Brigham Young

There Never Was A Time

There never was a time
That there were not Gods.
Or men and women
Facing their mortal lot.
There is not a space
That one can hide.
From their laws
That rule above all.
We are all in subjection
To their will.
In the Eternal worlds
This you will feel.
When you are allotted
Your Eternal prize.

And see the sparkle
That shines in their eyes.
If you did good,
The prize you will win.
But for he who chose sin,
Well, I'd hate to be him.

How many Gods there are, I do not know. But there never was a
time when there were not Gods and worlds, and when men were not
passing through the same ordeals that we are now passing through.
Brigham Young

No End

There is no end?
How can such I comprehend?
No end to race?
No end to matter?
No such thing as pure space,
Where nothing has a place?
No end to priesthood?
No end to Love?
No end to Glory?
No death above?
We will live forever and ever?
What will we do?
All these questions,
I haven't a clue!
Can you please tell me

W.W Phelps,
Do you?

To tell about empty space is to tell of a place where God
is not, and where the wicked might safely hide from his
presence. There is not such a thing as empty space.
Brigham Young

I want to be like Him

Oh how Great
Is my Father above,
Who teaches me
How to Love,
A love so pure,
That I gladly endure.
He's never wrong
He's always right,
He always says
Let us not fight,
Instead let me teach you
The ways of peace,
That if you follow,
You will never feel hollow.
Come little child
And follow my lead,
That you may learn
The road to follow.
You will feel

The storms and heat,
But just endure
And one day you will reach,
Where I am
You will find,
Is where you want to be
At the end of time.

God cares a lot more about who we are, and who we
are becoming, than about who we once were.
Dale G. Renlund

———

Prophets Of Old And Of Days To Come

Kicked out from town to town,
They travelled the land up and down.
Trying to find someone to teach.
Trying to find a soul that they could reach.
Of the Gospel that saved their lives,
That gave them a joy they couldn't deny.
Oh how often they would cry,
As people would reject them and God deny.
But harder and harder they would try,
Because of the love which they possessed.
The love with which, God, them blessed.
So in Gods name, they testify,
Of the truth, they dared not lie.
No matter the mountains they had to climb.

No matter the storms that they would find.
They persisted and they pursued,
To the rod, they stayed true.
They would hold on tight, and continue to fight.
For they knew true, that what they taught was right.

As I am blessed now to pray with apostles and prophets, I
find among these modern-day leaders of the saviours church
the same characteristic's that describe captain Moroni
in the Book of Mormon: these are men whose hearts
swell with thanksgiving to God for the many privileges
and blessings which he bestows among his people.
David A Bednar

I Want To Be A Wild Man Like Enoch Of Old

I want to be a wild man like Enoch of old!
Who taught the Gospel true and bold!
Everywhere he went, people revered!
Some fled in fright whilst others cheered!
There were some, that would mock and jeer.
But when Enoch spoke, they had to cover their ears.
They could not handle his words of truth.
For the spirit testified to all that they were true.
Some cowered and others ran,
But there was not one who mocked, that could stand.
That ground would shake as he roared words true.
Straight from heaven, these words came, the people knew.

Evil men changed their hearts, while others just fell apart,
In doom and despair as they began to comprehend,
That God is real and is a really big deal.
Oh how some mourned as he blew his horn,
His manner of speaking, causing them to become torn.
They knew not what to do because they loved evil.
But nothing could they do, because of that which Enoch knew.
He convinced many, of the ways of God.
Taught them in time to become like him.
Then one day, God took them away.
Up to Heaven to live with him.
I want to be a wild man like Enoch of old.
So that I may teach the Gospel, true and bold.

A man filled with the Love of God, is not content with
blessing his family alone, but ranges through the whole
world, anxious to bless the whole human race.
Joseph Smith

What Can I Do???

Father, please tell me, what I can do,
To be of a great service to you.
What must I learn?
What must I do?
To help these people, who haven't a clue?
Surely there is a way, to make them understand?
Surely there is a way to make them comprehend?

You cannot make them Son,
They have to want to.
They have their agency,
To listen or reject you.
Not everybody, will become as me.
Only those, who seek me diligently.
You can however master all my teachings,
And power will I give, to make you convincing.
How about I teach you the manner of speaking,
That I taught to your hero, Enoch of old?
And how about I twinkle you, that you may also glow?
Be patient Son and continue learning.
And know that I love you
And never stop yearning.
Your desires are righteous,
So continue this path,
And one fine day,
By my side you will stay.

And it came to pass that Enoch went forth in the land,
among the people, standing upon the hills and the high
places, and cried with a loud voice, testifying against their
works, and all men were offended because of him.
And they came forth to hear him, upon the high places, saying
unto the tent keepers: Tarry ye here and keep the tents, while we
go yonder to behold the seer, for he prophesieth, and there is a
strange thing in the land; a wild man hath come among us.
And it came to pass when they heard him, no man laid hands on him;
for fear came on all them that heard him; for he walked with God.
Moses 6:37-39

I Want To Be Like Enoch

What an adventure is Grace!
Bestowed upon me so I can end this race!
I want to be like Enoch!
Whom was worthy to walk with God!
Mastered the ways,
That to him God gave!
Then inspired a city to learn them too!
Transfigured were the people!
And the buildings too!
I want to be like Enoch
Whom was worthy to walk with God!
To master the ways,
That to me God gave!

If we want to be as righteous as the city of Enoch, we need
to quit comparing ourselves to others, to quit competing,
and quit fighting, and end racism. They were saved for their
charity, their Christlike love, for loving their neighbours, for
their service. It will all workout as we serve Christ the Lord.
Courtney Castrey

I Want To Be Like!

I want to be like Elijah who called down fire from the Heavens!
I want to be like Enoch from whom Giants fled! Mountains tumbled!
Rivers turned! And trees churned!

I want to be like Nephi whose faith was stronger then diamonds!
I want to be like Solomon who chose wisdom before gold!
I want to be like John the most beloved of God!
I want to be like Job who had enough faith to pet a lion!
I want to be like Jacob who had angels minister unto he!
And even saw through the veil into Eternity!
I want to be like Alma whom from prisons fall!
I want to be like them all!

Seek me diligently and ye shall find me.
Ask and ye shall receive.
Knock and it shall be opened unto you.
D&C 88:63

Beware The Snare

Be careful not to wonder
Like the rat to the cheese.
Who thought to himself,
I can do this with ease.
He prayed not for council
Nor did he listen to the spirit.
Who warned him of such dangers
And there'd be consequences if he did it.
Oh how he now, wishes that he,
Listened closely, and carefully.
To that soft gentle whisper,
That told him not to do it.
Oh why! Oh why!

When I knew it! I knew it!
That if I partook,
I would surely die.
But it looked so good
I just wanted to try!
I thought I knew better
Than what I was taught.
Oh thank goodness my soul,
Jesus bought.

You live in a world where moral values have, in great measure,
been tossed aside, where sin is flagrantly on display, and where
temptations to stray from the straight and narrow path surround you
Thomas S Monson

The Power Of God

The Power of God
Can only be beheld!
I would tell you about it
But you would tell me to go to Hell.
You wouldn't believe me
If I told you what he could do,
You would look at me
Like you haven't a clue.
And I would sigh in my heart
Oh dear poor you,
For you understand not
That it has the Power

To change even you!
A Power that can Strengthen,
Heal and Renew.
Even the least
Can become
As Great as he is!
He who rules this Universe
And others as well!
Who comprehends the Eternities!
And my problems as well!
Who Loves and cares for us individually,
Teaches me to grow
Spiritually, emotionally and mentally!
To be better and better!
Each and every day!
Until that wonderful moment
That I will hear him say!
It is time to come home
To claim your right!
To have your own throne
And to rule by my Might!
And I will cry out!
With Joy and delight!
Thank you Heavenly Father
For helping me
To choose the Right!

True change, permanent change can come only through the healing,
cleansing, and enabling power of the atonement of Jesus Christ.
Russell M Nelson

Heaven

I often wonder, I often ponder,
What it would be like
To live near he.
I heard that the roads are paved with gold!
And the palaces saturated with gems untold!
The walls are coloured with crystals unknown!
And a wave of peace doth fill this home!
The flowers dance and sing songs of romance!
The cities stretch beyond the eye!
But blend in well with the countryside!
Everywhere you look there are berries to pick!
Tons of spots to have a picnic!
Skyscrapers fill the bright blue sky!
The heights thereof, invisible to the naked eye!
The roar of waterfalls all around!
As they beat upon this mighty ground!
Canyons so large and magnificent!
With colours so intense and sufficient!
Always a gentle breeze in your ear!
And the presence of God you always feel near!
Oh Great God thank you for letting me see!
What it's like to be living in heaven with thee!

The ultimate treasures on Earth and in Heaven
are our children and our posterity.
Dallin H Oaks

Everything Is Better In Heaven

Let me tell you of a secret!
But only if you promise
That you will keep it!
Did you know?
Have you been told?
That everything is better
Up in heaven!
Every feeling!
Every colour!
Every passion!
No matter,
How intense I tell you now!
That up in heaven
It is better!
Every wonderful experience
To be gained in mortality,
Is but a taste,
A portion of that which is in Eternity!
So I don't know about you
But as for me my dear friends,
I can't wait to return to live in Heaven again!
So study hard the words of the prophets!
For by learning their wisdom
You will surely profit!

Now let me tell you a secret, I do not know that you have ever
thought of it, the most intense passion of love that can be felt

in these mortal tabernacles, is nothing more than a foretaste of
the love the eternities are full of in the kingdom of our God
Brigham Young

Oh Dear Me

Is this healthy for my brain?
Have I lost my mind and gone insane?
The wonders of Eternity doth consume me,
It's mighty flames are burning right through me!
All I can hear is its overwhelming roar!
With an unquenchable thirst, all I want is more!
Please God, please pour,
Unto me knowledge, until there is left no more!
I cannot sleep, I cannot eat,
All I want, is to partake of this feast!
Please make thine mysteries known!
For I cannot rid myself of this taste of home.

No message appears in scripture more times, in
more ways than "Ask and Ye shall receive."
Boyd K Packer

Jesus

His very stare shaketh my Soul,
He possesses a power I cannot behold.
He is so gentle and emotionally stable.
So empowered and extremely able.
How it frightens me to think that he was just like us!
In a tabernacle of flesh and bones,
Now Immortalised and Glorified and Perfected in every way,
His reward for wisely spending all of his days.
He used his agency to surpass us all,
The most intelligent above all.
Came to Earth and conquered all,
Overcame the world, without so much as a fall.
Went from Grace to Grace until he received,
The fullness of The Father and became one with he.
Now a Lord God, Exalted, one day you will see.

The spirits of men were not equal. They may have had an equal start,
and we know they were all innocent in the beginning; but the right of
free agency which was given to them enabled some to outstrip others.
Joseph F Smith Jr

———— ∿⦁◦⦿◦⦿◦∿ ————

The Trail Of Treasures

Following the trail of treasures,
I am taken far away.
Heavenly Father shows me new lands,

In which are fun to play.
All the same things doth he show me,
Only in a better way.
The world is a different place now,
That Heavenly Father is lighting the way.

Our goal is to achieve Eternal life! This is
the greatest goal in the world!
Spencer W Kimball

Where? Oh Where?

Where is the road? Where is the way?
I search and I search all day and everyday,
But still I have not found, not even the Gate.
How long oh Great God before I may,
Walk the same paths as did they?
The prophets of old who lived long ago,
Who now enjoy, a happiness untold.
Nevertheless! I will continue to try!
For I must thread the needles eye,
Before it is my time to die.

Strait is the gate and narrow is the way which leaders
unto life and few there be that find it.
Mathew 7:14

Out Of This World

Tablets of Gold and pillars of fire!
Men who stand in the dens of lions!
Angels whose roar shaketh the ground!
Treasure untold that I have found!
What is this that I have stumbled upon?
A God so Holy that even cares when I am down.
Angels sing and worship him!
Singing praises and glorious hymns!
Who is this that was once a man,
Now a God with for me a plan?

As man now is God once was, as God now is man can become.
Lorenzo Snow

What Will Be Of Me?

Will I stand the test of time?
Will that Great reward one day be mine?
Will I conquer all there is?
Overcome the world and inherit all there is?
Will I be strong enough?
To endure the storms and weather so rough?
Will I be able to sit with the Greats!
Like Moses and Abraham or Joseph of late?
Oh Great God what is to be my fate?

He that overcometh shall inherit all things.
Revelations 21:7

Help

How long my God before I am free?
How long my God before I am like thee?
How long my God will you suffer me,
To endure this hell of mortality?
I know it is never more than I can bear,
But such torment comes upon me
As my heart strings you tear.
I wish to conquer them once and for all,
But I am weak and constantly I fall.
Please help me Great God to conquer all.

You will have all kinds of trials to pass through. And it is
quite as necessary for you to be tried as it was for Abraham
and other men of God, and (said he) God will feel after
you, and He will take hold of you and wrench your very
heart strings, and if you cannot stand it you will not be fit
for an inheritance in the Celestial Kingdom of God.
Joseph Smith

There Is Light At The End Of The Tunnel

As I continue to claw my way out of hell,
I hear the warning bells ring.
And the voice of lucifer screams in my ears,
Don't let that boy win!
But I must keep fighting on toward this Heavenly scene,
Where I see my Heavenly Parents!
And with them Angels Sing!

Pray always that you may come off conqueror!
D&C 10:5

———⟋⟍⟋⟍⟋⟍———

What Happened To You?

Dear Satan,
Do you know how many souls are lost?
Because of your hatred
And your wickedness,
Or how many have been inflicted
With such a great sickness,
A sorrow heart
Filled with emptiness.
Is this your bidding?
Is this your will?
What causes you to be so evil?
I wonder why every night,

That you could possibly
Take such delight,
In causing your Brothers
And Sisters as well,
To follow the path
That leads to hell.
Oh can't you hear
The Heavens mourn,
The mighty family you have torn.
Is this what you really wanted
Your Great name shamed
Forever tamed.
You were the Son of the Morning!
One of the most beautiful!
Now we all wonder,
What happened to you?

In the war in heaven the devil advocated absolute
eternal security at the sacrifice of our freedom.
Ezra Taft Benson

—∞∽◦⌒◯⌒◦∾∞—

Be Gone Satan!

Be gone Satan!
Back to your home.
Go away!
And leave me alone.
You chose your sentence,
By thinking you could force repentance.

You wanted to deny us our freedom
To choose our path,
You wanted to force us
To do your part.
To take away our agency
And follow your heart.
You challenged the Father
And led many astray,
You caused the mourning of Mothers
You left Heaven in disarray.
Now look where you are
And what you are doing.
You fail to repent
And instead still,
Gather armies
To do your will.
You became a Devil
Through your evil ways,
It looks like forever
This way you will stay.
Cursed to spend forever
In misery,
As miserable a creature
As can be.

Agency allows us to be tested and tried to see whether or not we will endure to the end and return to our Heavenly Father with honour. Agency permits us to make faithful, obedient choices that strengthen us so that we can lift and strengthen others.
Robert D Hales

My Time Shall Come

Mountains shall I mold!
And rivers shall I carve!
Canyons shall I chisel!
And forests shall I seed!
Animals shall I breed!
Both on land and in the sea!
The sky I shall paint upon!
Every shape of cloud!
And fill it with birds for all to see!
Then the creeping and crawling things I will need!
But not the mosquitos!
I will leave them out I think!
Then I will send my children!
To go forth and multiply!
And teach to them the Gospel!
As my Father did for I!

Never forget who you are!

What Would I Do?

If I were to give up,
What would I do?
Where would I go?
Where else can I learn of you?
Where else can I go

To find my way home?
What else will stand at the end of time?
What else matters?
What else is real?
Can you tell me of a better deal?

If we hold tightly to the word of God, we will
remain on the pathway to Eternal Life.
L Tom Perry

The Gods Are Right!

From the lowest Hell
He took me in,
Washed away
And cleansed my sins.
Taught me the ways
Of righteousness,
So that someday
I might dwell with him!
The ways of Joy
And happiness!
The way to conquer
All of your sadness.
Just listen close
And you will learn,
What he has to offer
Will make you yearn!
For more and more,

Everyday,
You will know
That this is the way!
The way that you want
Your kids to live,
The way that you want
Your world to live.
To be morally right
Come on, why fight?
I declare this now
That The Gods
Are right!

I testify that the tender mercies of the Lord are real
and that they do not occur randomly or merely by
coincidence. Often, the Lords timing of his tender mercies
helps us to both discern and acknowledge them.
David A Bednar

Gratitude

Grant me thine power that truth I may roar.
That Souls I may teach and hearts I might reach.
I wish to be thine most profitable servant,
Please teach me dear Lord that this I may be.
Grant me the honour of servitude to thee,
That I may express my gratitude truly.
For all you have done I cannot repay,
Not in a million years, never, no way.

But try I will everyday,
That a bit of this debt I might repay.

To the Lord Jesus, who bought us with a great
price, we owe an undying debt of gratitude.
Marion G Romney

———~~∽◦◟◟◠◟◠◝◟◦~~———

Unimaginable

Please help me Dear God
Of this I pray.
Each and everyday
That I might be shown the way.
Show me what
I need to do,
So that I can come live with you.
In the spheres that dwell so high,
That even my imagination,
There cannot fly.
Of this place,
All I know,
Is that I,
Really want to go.
Of its beauty the spirit testifies.
Which causes me,
To sometimes cry.
Because I know,
That God cannot lie.

Exaltation is our goal. Discipleship is our journey.
Dieter F Uchtdorf

———❧∽◦∼◦∼◦∽❧———

To Be With You Again

Oh my Lord
Oh my Father
Give me all
That I require,
To be like thee
In every way,
So that I may dwell
With thee some day.
Teach me all
That I must do,
Show me what
I must become,
So that I
Can live with you,
And my God,
The mighty Son.
When this journey
I've completed,
And my sins
Become depleted,
When I'm clean
And a perfected being,
Praises to thee
Forever will I sing.

I will love
As you have loved
Forevermore
Outwardly I will pour,
All my love,
To all and all.

When we choose to follow Christ, we choose to be changed.
Ezra Taft Benson

—⁓◦⌒⌒⌒⌒◦⁓—

The Refiners Fire

The fire burns and continues to rage,
It's flames soar with an overpowering roar,
It is so painful, yet it leaves me wanting more.
Its heat burns at such a degree,
That it melts away my impurities,
Slowly refining me into Heavens pedigree.
In the end it will be well worth it,
But as for now, I must suffereth it.

How could there be refining fires without our enduring some heat?
Neal A Maxwell

—⁓◦⌒⌒⌒⌒◦⁓—

Grace

O Grace you are so sweet,
You I wish to give a kiss.
You never miss,
You always know!
Just which way
I should go!

With the gift of God's Grace, the path of discipleship
does not lead backward, it leads upward.
Dieter F Uchtdorf

Please Set Me Right

Please set me right my Lord,
My sins keep me awake all night.
I want to be like you,
Filled with your love and light.
You are so gentle and your love is unknown,
But to those with the deepest desire,
To one day see home.

Our journey on the path is personal and well lit with the Saviors love.
Rosemary Wixom

Feeling Rich

In endless streams of mercy doth I swim,
As my Father and Brother help me to win,
The battle for my soul so I can act for myself,
And one day be showered with endless wealth.
Treasures of a Godly love doth I seek,
For rich is he with whom God doth meet.
The fullness of his character is what I chase,
As I journey in sackcloth huddled at his feet.
The warmth of his love keeps out the cold,
Oh how I wish of this Love you could know.

Where and when we feel the closeness of the
Saviour depends on each of us.
Henry B Eyring

Mountains Of Love

Guided by the God I love,
I journey through mortality,
In search of his promised prize,
The one and only,
Eternal 'LIFE!'
Mountains of Love doth I climb,
Oceans of mercy doth I swim,
All I can say is that
I love him!

Spiritual guidance is received when needed, in
the Lords time and according to his will.
Quentin L Cook

So Divine

He sought me as a stranger wondering the wilderness,
And gave to me living water to drink.
It filled my heart and I thirsted no more,
But yet more and more did he pour.
Gave me shelter from the cold,
And taught me a love that I never had known.
A Godly love so divine,
It makes me proud to call him mine.

He therefore knows our struggles, our heartaches, our temptations
and our sufferings. And because of this, his Atonement empowers
him to succour us - to give us the strength to bear it all.
Dallin H Oaks

My Heart

Endless mercy never ceasing,
Praise the Lord for giving me,

The teachings of Eternity,
That make me so very happy.
Safety from the storms
And shelter from the rain,
He is able to succour all of my pain.
Take my heart Lord and please heal it,
For your courts above please take and seal it.

Because of his atonement, the Saviour has the power to
succour - to help - every mortal pain and affliction.
Dallin H Oaks

—◦◦◦◦◦◦◦◦◦◦◦◦◦◦—

Praises To My God And King

Mountains of redeeming love
Surround me from above.
Like a beggar, I praise the debtor,
For he saved me with his love.
Endless mercy sweeps over me,
Slowly setting my Heart free.
I know now that he truly loves me,
For I feel it burning within me.
Songs I sing now, are Heart felt,
Praises to my God and King.

I know that my redeemer lives.

—◦◦◦◦◦◦◦◦◦◦—

Singing Praises All The Way

Oh Sire, with your fire,
Redeem my soul today.
For I am troubled everyday,
By all my wicked ways.
With your kindness and your love,
Oh won't you guide the way.
I will follow, where you go,
Singing praises all the way.

He is our Saviour and Redeemer, our advocate with
the Father. He is our Exemplar and our strength.
He is the light which shineth in darkness.
Thomas S Monson

———⁓⁓◦⟲◦⟲⟩⟲◦⟨⟲⟩⟲⟩⟲◦⟩◦⁓⁓———

Jesus Saved Me

Jesus saved me, from the fire of misery,
With his gentle ways.
With love and kindness, through his spirit,
He guides me through my days.
There's now no way, that I can deny,
Or ever turn away.
He lives to save his people, for he loves them,
And wishes them not to stray.
Now I sing songs of love and praise,
While looking forward to better days.

Gods ultimate purpose is our progress.
D Todd Christofferson

My Heart You Have Won

Sometimes I laugh, sometimes I cry.
Sometimes I just lie there and wonder why.
Why would God save a wretch like me,
Why would God want to speak with me.
All the things that I have done,
And yet he still wants to call me Son.
Father all I can say to you,
Is thank you for all that you do.
I will never ever leave,
For this you must know,
My heart you have won,
My countenance now glows.

No God does not need us to love him. But
oh, how we need to love God!
Dieter F Uchtdorf

When You Really Have God!

Who needs a wife when you have God!
The all supreme Master of the Iron Rod!
The ruler of universes so majestically grand!
The author of this wondrous beautifully executed plan!
The keeper of mysteries of all things untold!
The lover of Goddesses so beautiful and bold!
The creator of worlds without number I am told!
The shepherd who lovingly brought me into his fold!
The teacher to the instructions of the Gospel of Life!
The keeper of the Gate that leads me into Eternal Life!
I wouldn't trade this for the whole world!
Wait! What's that Father? You want to find me a girl?
Oh! Ok then!

Just Joking!

Tis A Joy To Learn The Gospel

Tis a Joy to learn the Gospel!
And feel the Holy Ghost!
Guide me and direct me
Toward the tree of life!
Whose fruits I have tasted!
Hunger I no more!
For wells of living water
Do quench my thirst some more!

Wisdom, knowledge and Power!
Is taught to me every hour!
Such Glory I never beheld
Such Love I never knew
As that poured down from heaven!
Making me anew!

To live with gratitude ever in our hearts is to touch Heaven!
Thomas S Monson

Such A Stranger You Have Been

Oh Love,
Such a stranger you have been.
Until now,
That I can feel you through him.
All day, and every day,
I can feel you from within.
Oh please keep coming
To visit me with him.
How perfect is his presence,
How strong is his strength,
How wonderful his embrace,
Each and every day
I yearn to see his face.
He is surely Lord!
He is surely King!
Such majesty is he!
To suffer and die for my sins.

He is family,
To me above all!
For truly has he proven,
Himself to be!
Never has he failed me,
Never has he lied,
Instead always,
He has been by my side.
He is God!
As this is what a God is!
Someone who possesses
A Love such as his!
One day I aim,
To be just like him!
Oh how I cry,
As he invites me in.

At times we may even feel insignificant, invisible, alone or
forgotten. But always remember, you matter to him!
Dieter F Uchtdorf

But A Taste

By praying unceasingly
Hour by hour,
I have come to know
Of his matchless Power.
Things not yet revealed
Have been shown to me,

Things that were once
A mystery.
Such as matters of history!
And secrets pertaining to Eternity!
And all the positives of humanity!
Such as Love!
Such as Passion!
Such depths of feeling!
And endless emotions!
Such wonders! Oh boy!
And this is but a taste
Of Heavenly joy!

Yea he that repenteth and exerciseth faith, and bringeth forth good works, and prayeth continually without ceasing – unto such it is given to know the mysteries of God; yea, unto such it shall be given to reveal things which never have been revealed; yea, and it shall be given unto such to bring thousands of souls to repentance, even as it has been given unto us to bring these our brethren to repentance.
Alma 26:22

So Happy!

I'm so Happy!
I feel so free!
Now that I keep the commandments
That God gave to me!
I feel his Love for me every day!
I feel it in so many ways!

How to describe it,
Is impossible to say!
Except that I can feel it
More and more
Everyday!

Happiness comes from living the way the Lord wants you to live!
Thomas S Monson

Oh Won't You?

God I pray to you this day
For an understanding heart
To Love thy people,
That I may discern
Between good and evil.
You are God!
The Great Almighty!
Oh won't you hold
Onto me tightly!
Don't let me go
Down dark, dirty roads,
Help me to stay
On the straight and narrow,
My life to thee!
I pledge to follow!
Please open my eyes
That I may see,

The road to take
To become like thee!
My Great God!
The Almighty!

We choose who to follow.
Boyd K Packer

—⁓⚬⚭⚬⚮⚬⚭⚬⁓—

Who Art Thee?

Who art thee that carest for me?
Who art thee that with thine love sets me free?
Who art thee The Great High King of Heaven
to notice insignificant little me?
Oh Great Love of my heart! Who art thee?
Thine Spirit Ye send to encompass my sorrow,
Thy love when I am need you allow me to borrow.
Oh Great Love of my heart! Who art thee?
When I am lost you send me instruction to follow,
When I am lonely you rescue me from the hollow.
Oh Great Love of my heart! Who art thee?
Oh Great Love of my heart! Who art thee?

If the Kingdom of God is not first, it doesn't matter what's second.
Neal A Maxwell

—⁓⚬⚭⚬⚮⚬⚭⚬⁓—

My Story

Oh how happy the man
Who partakes of that tree,
Oh how filled that that man
His joy can be,
Oh how wonderful to know
God's Eternal mysteries,
Oh how wonderful to learn
How to escape that misery,
What an amazement
To understand,
He who loves,
And comprehends,
All my troubles
And all my sorrows
To him,
I forever will follow,
Forever will I dwell
In his presence and glory,
Forever and ever
This is my story!

1 Nephi 8

Revelation

Revelation is communication from on High!
Through it I am learning how to fly!
An entire mortality O my!
To learn how to be a Celestial King!
So that when I that Heavenly doorbell ring,
Gods voice I will hear sing!

Come in my Son it is time!
To claim your throne! To have your own!
You worked hard! You are deserving!
You beat the Devil! You came out first!
Can you not hear him your name curse!

The ability to qualify for, receive and act on personal revelation is
the single most important skill that can be acquired in this life.
Julie B Beck

———

One So Penitent

I feel like I am in the garden of Gathsemene.
As the weight of my sins burden me,
I can feel a thousand flames burning within me.
As Gods redeeming fire destroys the old me,
I am lightened as a feather
As I feel God forgiving me.

I rejoice of his intelligence
As the Power of his Grace changes me.
Scales fall from my eyes
As knowledge from Heaven awakens me.
I am guided slowly home
As the spirit whispers to me.
All of this is possible because of his Atonement,
Now how I treasure each and every moment.

Broken minds can be healed just the way broken
bones and broken hearts are healed.
While God is at work making those repairs, the rest of us
can help by being merciful, nonjudgmental and kind.
Jeffrey R Holland

He Has Won Me Over

Who knoweth these things
Save it be the penitent.
He who daily
Practices repentance.
For through sorrow,
Comes the joy I borrow.
From my Father on high,
Which often reasons me to cry.
Oh my God why did I have to sin?
Causing my brother to die from within,
Of a broken heart that tore even him.
The mightiest of all,
My Love did he win.

Please understand that the way back is not as hard as it
seems to you now. Satan wants you to think that it is
impossible. That is not true. The saviour gave his life so that
you can completely overcome the challenges you face
Richard G. Scott

Ammon And I

Day by day,
Hour by hour.
How I am comforted
By thy mighty power.
Snatched from my awful state,
Ye saved me before it was too late.
I was encircled by darkness and destruction
And it's everlasting chains.
Oh how the spirit of the Devil
Is far from tame.
Consigned me not
To an eternal despair.
Instead you showed me
Your kind, loving and generous mercy.
You showed me the ways
Of the Gods above.
And taught me to sing
With redeeming Love.
I cannot say the smallest part
That which I feel.
Except to you my God
I will kneel.

The Lord Jesus Christ can help us fix anything that needs
fixing in our lives through his atoning sacrifice.
M Russell Ballard

———— ∞∞∞∞∞∞∞ ————

Jesus Loves Me

Jesus Loves me this I know!
For he truly told me so!
This I know from my head to my toes!
That he loves me with all his Soul!

The Lord knows you personally and perfectly. He loves you.
D Todd Christofferson

———— ∞∞∞∞∞∞∞ ————

The Heavenly Warrior

As I march into war
Angels walk with me!
Sent by my Father
To bear me up swiftly!
Nothing can stop me!
Not the Devil himself,
Nor his angels
Who with him dwell,

In the darkest,
Deepest, Hell.
Filled with light
Sent from Heaven,
They flee in fright
At my very sight!
My very name
Keeps them awake at night!
They once beat me
In many battles,
But boy I tell you
I did fight!
And with Heavenly Fathers help,
I chose the right!
Now they flee in horror
With fists clenched tight!
Because they know
That Heavenly Father
Is holding me tight.

The men and women who desire to obtain seats in the Celestial
Kingdom will find that they must battle everyday.
Brigham Young

—⟋⟍⟋⟍⟋⟍⟋⟍—

Our Purpose

He knows everything!
Of this I testify!
Of my God I dare not lie!

For he lives!
He conquered all!
So he could learn,
To teach us not to fall!
For our sins
He suffered and died!
So that we could repent
And one day live again by Fathers side!
Should you choose this road to follow,
It is all uphill and the path straight and narrow!
Expect mountains to block your way!
But pray for God's Grace
So that you may,
Have the strength
To climb them everyday!
And pray for guidance
To be shown the way!
The road to travel,
That you might not stray!

Our path is uphill most days, but the help we
receive for the climb is literally divine
Jeffrey R Holland

The Way Back

My whole Soul he is healing
As my heart was once bleeding.
With fire is he redeeming,

All my sinful desires he is burning.
Oh my God what an extraordinary feeling!
This all started with me kneeling,
To my God with whom I was pleading,
For much saving I was needing.

Now such joy do I know!
More precious than coloured stones!
A joy that I can feel, flowing right through my bones!
Causing me to tremble,
When God causes me to remember.
All those years ago before we met.
When I was trapped, in Satans net.
Much have I to be thankful for!
For he wishes to give me all!
Such a Love I've never known.
He has upon my soul, grown.

When we stray - when we fall or depart from the way
of our Heavenly Father - the words of the prophets
tell us how to rise up and get back on track!
Dieter F Uchtdorf

———⁓⁓⚬⚬⚬⚬⚬⚬⚬⁓⁓———

One Chance

If I saw u tonight
Would I hide in fright,
Or would I rejoice
And scream out in delight!

Would I hug you
Would I kiss you
Would I utter
God I missed you!
Would I run to you
Or would I run from you,
Would I hide
Or would I cry,
Would I tell the truth
Or try to lie,
Would I jump
Would I shout,
Or would I be sad and would I pout,
Would I dance
Would there be a romance?
Or will I hear
You had your chance.

Be the same person you are in the dark, that you are in the light.
Thomas S Monson

The Ambience Of Heaven

The ambience is tranquil,
Of this you will feel,
When entering into Heaven,
A feeling oh so real.
You will remember
What you once enjoyed,

An over whelming feeling
Of inner peace inside.
A love so strong
All your worries will be gone!
Embraced by the father,
All his Love to you he will pour!
Congratulations little one,
You overcame the world!
Move along now
For this is just the door.

Every trial and experience you have passed
through is necessary for your salvation.
Brigham Young

—— ᨳᨳᨳᨳᨳ ——

Come And Learn

Your never too old
To come and learn
The beauties of what is to be,
So come my friend!
So come my foe!
And partake of a Love untold!
The Glory of God
And all of his friends
Who sit on their Exalted Thrones!
To us he extends
Through Jesus's hands,
The opportunity

For us to grow!
If you will come
Be humble and learn
Of such things you
Will come to know!
That God in Heaven
Can be a Father,
A Father to your soul!
He will nurture
And by his nature
You will learn
Of a life untold!
A life so supernal!
A life of Eternal
Treasures and Wealth unknown
To the natural eye.
For the natural eye,
Such things
Cannot behold!
So come my friend!
So come my foe!
And learn of this Love untold!

We need to learn how God speaks to us
individually, for he comes to us as we are.
Michael Wilcox

The Pleasure Is Mine

He who doth not love you,
Truly doth not know you.
For you are so beautiful,
And simply irresistible.
With a character so pure,
Just to be near is a joy.
To you my friend,
I will forever revere.
Never will I forget,
What you have done.
Praises forever,
To The Father and Son.

Think of the purest, most all-consuming love you can
imagine. Now multiply that love by an infinite amount.
That is the measure of Gods love for your.
Dieter F Uchtdorf

Sigh

Your Love is so sweet,
Your Love is so tender.
Oh how my God,
To you I surrender.
The world I have forsaken,
Your Kingdom doth I seek.

I long for the day,
When we will finally meet.
How will it be I sometimes wonder.
To meet a God who tears asunder.
Nations and Kingdoms, planets and suns.
And every battle, he hath won.
Extinguishes Suns with but a breath.
Worlds created by a command,
Simply wills, and it is done.
When armies see him, they turn and run.
Even shines brighter than the mighty sun.
Yet being with him is so much fun.
Laughs and jokes, giggles and makes fun.
Has the best sense of humour.
How I wish I could see you sooner.

Coming unto the Lord is not a negotiation, but a surrender.
Neal A Maxwell

Here's To A Better You

What are you going to say,
When you meet him one day,
Will you cower
In the presence of his mighty power?
Or will you feel,
Of a peace so surreal.
Tell me,
Do you look forward to that hour?

Are you expecting a reward?
Or to be smitten by his sword?
If it be the later, then rejoice with me now!
For the time is not yet,
His arms are still open!
He waits to receive you,
In the very moment!
That you decide to change your ways,
To repent of your sins,
And do away with your evil days.
He will forgive you if you truly desire.
Your soul he will redeem with the refiners fire.
Your wounds he will heal,
And your mind renew.
And Grace he will give
To strengthen and aid you.
But only after you do
All that you can do.
And what will be,
Eventually,
Will be one like he,
Hopefully.
If you strive,
And not just survive.
Eternal life
Will be your prize.

Someday you and I will each have an individual face
to face interview with the Saviour himself.
Wendy W Nelson

Dearest Father, Dearest Brother

Dearest Father, dearest Brother.
How with Love,
Doth you smother,
Me every day,
In the gentlest of ways,
As I keep trying,
Like you to behave.
So many blessings you bestow.
There is no way
I could possibly know,
All that you do,
I haven't a clue,
All that I know is that
I love you.

It simply isn't possible to be a disciple of someone you don't know.
Sheri Dew

To My Father

Your wisdom is a pleasure to rely on!
Your ways so joyous to learn!
Your thoughts an honour to know!
And your Love is so sweet to my Soul!
I love to hear the whispers in my ear,
Of those things I need to improve,

So that one day, you will let me glow as bright as you!
So I thank you for gently persuading me,
To do all that I must do,
For making hard things easy,
And giving me the strength to do.
I can only say that if it wasn't for you,
I wouldn't know what I would do,
So here's a big thanks to you
For teaching me all of the rules.

When we keep the commandments, our lives will be
happier, more fulfilling and less complicated.
Thomas S Monson

One Day

My God,
Your ways are Wise!
Your purposes are Glorious!
Because of you
My Heart is Joyous!
I wish to learn of all your ways!
So in your church here will I stay!
Please bless with time,
The time i will need,
To prepare my heart and soul
To be ready to meet,
Up in Heaven
With you and Mother

But most of all
With my beloved Brother.

This life is the time for men to prepare to meet God.
Alma 34:32

———•~••~•~•••~•———

Might, Mind, Heart And Strength

With all my might, I fight for you.
With all my mind, I learn of you.
With all my Heart, I love you.
And with all my strength, I run to you.
I will fight for the freedoms and liberties
That you desire us to have.
I will learn of all your laws,
So that with you I may be heir.
I love you simply because you are beautiful,
And I run to you because you are wonderful.
These words do not describe,
Even a portion of what I feel inside.
A feeling that consists
Of a pure Heavenly bliss.
That engulfs my soul as the morning mist.
Of this I testify,
That you saved me from the darkest abyss.

The first great commandment of all Eternity is to love
God with all of our Heart, Might, Mind and Strength.

But the first great truth of all Eternity is that God loves
us with all of his Heart, Might, Mind and Strength.
Jeffrey R Holland

O

O the Spirit of God!
So soft, so gentle,
So kind, so sweet,
So giving, so liberal,
So great, so merciful,
So sincere, so wonderful,
So generous, so noble,
O the Spirit of God!

The Holy Ghost can do for us physically, emotionally, mentally and
intellectually what no man-made remedy can begin to duplicate.
Linda K Burton

Goodbye And Hello

Oh my God!
Oh my King!
With your help

This battle I will win!
Mountains will I climb!
Trials will I conquer!
This world I will overcome!
This battle I will have won!
Darkness will flee!
From all around me!
For filled with your light I shall be!
Clothed in Eternal Glory!
Granted to me from on High!
As to my sinful ways,
I say goodbye.

God never loses sight of our Eternal potential, even when we do.
Sister Stephens

—⁓⁓⁓—

Woe Is Me. Woe Is Me.

Woe is me. Woe is me.
Oh dear Lord,
Where is she?
I cannot find
The one I want to marry.
I search and I search
But to no avail.
I cannot find a woman
To my travail.
A woman who Loves
And fears the Lord.

A woman who lives
To one day see God.
A woman who wants to reach
The highest degree.
A woman who wants
To go there with me.
A woman who abides by all Gods laws.
A woman who knows
Exactly what she was created for.
A woman who understands the Gospel
And where it came from.
A woman taught wisdom
By God himself.
A virtuous woman who has no price.
A woman who seeketh
To choose the right.
A woman that in her
I see Life!
A woman worthy
To call my wife!

There is this one Goddess. Actually there are so
many! But there is this one Goddess.

A Most Important Message

I would describe him to you,
But you wouldn't believe it to be true.
You would say no way,

And perhaps even tell me to go away.
And then you would hear me say,

Why don't you find out for yourself?
How do I do that? You might ask.
To which I would reply,
Seek my friends and you will find!
But you better hurry, before you run out of time!
You only have this life to prove yourself!
This is your test, your probation,
And it is but only, for a short duration.
What you achieve in mortality,
Will determine how you spend your Eternity.
So come unto him, and surrender from within.
By getting baptised into his living church,
The Church that bears his name boldly.
The Church which holds his authority,
To perform baptisms and other ordinances,
Such as Sealings and Eternal marriages.
The Church of Jesus Christ of Later Day Saints.
Then once you enter in the gates,
Hurry and master the scriptures before it gets too late.
We are told to be as perfect as he,
By trying our hardest then asking for help you see!
He will endow you with Power from on high!
This is Grace,
And it is essential to he who wishes to see his face.
For no unclean thing can enter in,
So repent we must, to be free from sin.
But beware for he knoweth our hearts,
And only the truly penitent, win.

None but the truly penitent are saved.
Alma 42:24
Why? Because you cannot teach somebody who doesn't want to learn.

Coming Home

As I pray
And I ponder
Oh Mighty God
You make me wonder,
What it's like
To live with you,
Up in Heaven
With Mother too!
I know I would like it
Just because of you!
But how much better
Now I know that there is two!
So prepare my mansion!
Because I'm coming home!
As soon as I'm ready
To sit on my Throne!
So hold the door open
Because I'm holding steadfast
To the iron rod,
That I may
Come home at last!

Everyone loses his or her way at some point, to some degree. It is
the atoning sacrifice of the saviour that can return us home.
M Russell Ballard

Mysteries!

Mysteries! Mysteries!
I know the Mysteries!
Do you want to know?
Do you want to hear?
Mysteries! God's Greatest Mysteries!
Quick! Lend me your ear!
Do you want me to tell you?
Are you ready? Quick come here!
Oh wait. Sorry.
They are not lawful for you to hear!

If thou shalt inquire, thou shalt know mysteries
which are Great and Marvelous!
D&C 6:11

I Wish

I wish I glew as bright as an angel,
That I might convince all of these people,
That God is real and does hear all,
For his angels are all around recording all.
I would tell them with a voice of thunder,
To change their ways or they will end up down under.
Convincing I would be for their own sakes,
So that they may awake before it grows too late.
I would help them to understand,
Our Great God's loving plan.
And that he wishes them a helping hand,
In becoming so much more than just a man.
For he wishes us all the Greatest of destinies,
To grow and develop to become just as he!
A Mighty God who was once just a man,
Now Exalted in yonder Heavens,
Can you understand???
It goes on forever, Father helping Son,
So that one day together, they might be one.
One in heart, mind and purpose,
To what end do you suppose?
To help future generations to become as they,
One in Heart, mind and purpose,
Forever and ever,
To dwell in righteousness.

As man now is, God once was, as God now is, man may become.
President Snow

We Are The Nobility Of Heaven

I am a King
Of royal descent!
Foreordained to win
This war I was sent!
To come off conquerer
And to overcome all!
To learn Gods ways
And to master them all!
So that I may inherit
All that is his!
This is my birth right
And of this,
I dream every night!
Of that Great day
That is set in my sights!
No wind can blow me
Off my course!
And although they rush me,
No devils can crush me!
For my Fathers Mighty Hand have I taken!
And nothing can stop me!

We were born to be Kings and Queens! Then Gods and Goddesses!

How Great And Wonderful

How Great and Wonderful
To have a friend in you!
How Great and Wonderful
To have a friend so true!
You pick me up
When I am feeling blue!
You teach me of things
Which I had not a clue!
Oh my dear God
This feels to good to be true!
How Great and Wonderful
To have a friend in you!

I testify that he is utterly incomparable in what he is, what
he knows, what he has accomplished and what he has
experienced. Yet, movingly, he calls us his friends.
Neal A Maxwell

Fairy Tales Can Come True!

Day by day!
Grace to Grace!
One fine day
When I have won this race,
I will behold
Thy Glorious face!

Forever I will dwell
In your presence and glory!
Forever and ever!
This will be my story!

Happily ever after is not something found only in fairy
tales. You can have it! Your own wondrous story has
already begun. Your once upon a time is now.
Dieter F Uchtdorf

Such Joy Can Come From Applying The Gospel

What joy there is in being happy!
What Happiness there is in Joy!
What life there is in Love!
What Love there is in Life!
What lessons to be learned from trouble!
Oh how I'm not going to let anyone pop my bubble!
Impenetrable will I be!
For all the world to see!
I declare this boldly now!
For tis my Destiny!
My God to whom I serve!
I pledge my life to thee!
He sent me here to Earth!
To Grow in mortality!
One day I will be Exalted!
And inherit all that he has!

Such treasures one can only dream off!
But never ever grasp!
Will be given to me!
By his Majesty!

Even in our trials we can experience joy and peace.
Robert D Hales

———∿∿◦◖⦿◗◖⦿◗◦∿∿———

Your Ways

Your ways are like the sound
Of breaking waves upon the shore.
Your voice can be as calm
As the harmonious melody of a choir.
Or as destructive
As the roar of the fiercest thunder.
Your love, words cannot describe.
And from your face, no man can hide.

We must constantly remind ourselves that he is God and we are not.
Jeffrey R Holland

———∿∿◦◖⦿◗◖⦿◗◦∿∿———

Nigh! Nigh!

My transformation is nigh complete!
So evil beware!
Prepare yourselves to flee in despair!
As I shine the rays of Heaven
The darkness must flee!
For darkness cannot stand the presence of light!
From it, it must flee!
And I tell you now that my light burns bright!
Thanks to my Heavenly Father who is teaching me the right!
I am almost ready to enforce his Might!

Darkness cannot persist in the presence of light.
Boyd K Packer

I Want To Glow

Perfection is my goal!
I wish to be made whole!
I want to receive the fullness of the Father!
All of his qualities, all that he is!
To be worthy to be called,
One of Heavens Royalties!
Having proven to him,
The fierceness of my loyalty!
My countenance will shine!
Brighter than the sun!

Of him I will declare!
As my feet float through the air!

To be worthy does not mean to be perfect.
Gerrit W Gong

He Loves Me

Slowly but surely I conquer he,
The devil who desires me an endless misery.
He doth try, and try and try and try.
But to no avail, in the end,
He is destined to fail.
For as surely as I stand before you
The Lord lives!
He loves me and Eternal life desires to give!
Rejoices at my desire to learn his will!
An Eternal reward receive I surely will!

Satan does not want you to think you can change. He
will try to convince you that all is lost. That is a lie.
You can return. You can repent. You can be pure and
Holy because of the Savior's infinite atonement.
Elaine S Dalton

Cursed

When Ye are cursed,
Ye will know not
That Ye are cursed.
Of beauty and wonder
Ye will not know.
Things of divine natures
Will be but strangers.
You will thrive
On living in danger.
Love and passion
Will be out of fashion.
Evil will be good
And good will be evil.
So do not stray
From the straight and narrow.
Brothers and sisters
This is the path to follow.
Come and learn how to love
Or forever you will remain
Miserable and cursed,
For Eternal life you will not attain,
And you will never have this opportunity again.

This is our one and only chance at mortal life - here and now.
I believe that among the greatest lessons we are to learn in
this short sojourn upon the earth are lessons that help us
distinguish between what is important and what is not.
Thomas S Monson

What A Beautiful God

Healed from pain.
Redeemed from stain.
Strengthened through Grace.
Loved by your beautiful face.
Taught by your wisdom,
On how to win this race.
So that come that day,
With you, I will have a place.
In the Kingdom of our Father
Forever in your Love,
In the place prepared for me above.

If healing doesn't come in this life, it will come there after.
Boyd K. Packer

I Love The Truth!

I love the truth!
It sets me free!
Knowing that I,
Am not accountable to thee!
I thank God for this!
Because you are nothing like he!
Quick to throw tantrums, getting mad and angry.
Learn the laws and embrace them all!
Or go tell God that his plan is flawed.
Learn the rules, and master them all,

For he that is guilty of one, is guilty of all.
And remember to be kind and gracious,
To one and all,
Because we don't become champions,
Without a couple of falls.

For whosoever shall keep the whole law, and yet
offend in one point, he is guilty of all.
James 2:10

My Name Call

Suffered the pains of the damnedest.
Raised from the dust by the Grandest.
I testify of his Might!
That he cannot loose a fight!
With wisdom and intellect beyond our own!
He is clearly like nobody I have ever known.
His thoughts soar higher than my imagination!
His ways are like a permanent vacation!
Taught by my Saviour to win this fight!
Yoked with him my burdens are made light.
With Joy I cry out in delight!
As I learn to master each and every right.
He holds my hand as I journey the fog,
He shows me the ways of the Iron Rod.
Gave me to eat, the fruits of the tree,
That leads into Life in Eternity.
Of which I tasted and cried and cried,
When in that moment I realised I had died.

I realised all that I had missed,
That I had at home in Heavens bliss!
Never again will I fall!
For he is teaching me to conquer all!
And one fine day when I have mastered them all,
I will hear the Saviour, my name call.

We were not put on this earth to fail but to succeed gloriously!
Richard G Scott

Spiritual Surgery

Performed with precision,
My God operates on me,
Cutting away all the cancers
That have grown within me.
With hands so steady,
And with unchallengeable skill,
He is healing all of my ills,
And is preparing me to come and live with him.

The Church is not an automobile showroom - a place to put
ourselves on display so that others can admire our spirituality,
capacity, or prosperity. It is more like a service centre, where vehicles
in need of repair come for maintenance and rehabilitation.
Dieter F Uchtdorf

Fly! Fly!

From littleness to Greatness!
You cannot stop me!
For God's Mighty hand have I taken
And he doth lead me!
Devils still try to bring me down,
But with wisdom and guidance from above,
Right through them do I plough!
Everything that they throw in my way,
Just makes me stronger by the day!
All my mountains look like hills,
And all my storms turned into a drizzle.
Thanks be to God who reigns on High,
Who doth teaches even me,
How to fly!

The men and women who desire to obtain seats in the Celestial
Kingdom will find that they must battle everyday.
Brigham Young

True Love

In your arms
I am safe from harm
There is no place I would rather be,
Then in the embrace of your Majesty,
Surrounded by your love,

Continuously rained down on me.
So gentle like a dove
So genuine,
This indeed must be true love.

He values us, he loves us, each daughter of God is
beloved by him and he desires to see us all succeed.
Neill F Marriott

God

From beginning to end,
All things doth he know.
Anything and everything,
Especially the secrets of your Soul.
All that is dark,
He will one day make known.
To be brought before the bar of God,
And to be sentenced by the laws of the Iron Rod.
The laws of Justice and Mercy,
Which grants Mercy unto the repentant,
And Justice to the rebellious.
All wrongs will be made right
To those who stood and fight,
And they will receive their Great reward
If they are found spotless before our Great God.
For these are they who sought diligently,
The wonders and teachings of the Eternities.
Learnt and mastered all that they had to do,
From their constant companion the Holy Ghost who,

Was sent to them from on very High,
Because of the lamb who was crucified.
They received him with open arms
And applied his teachings,
As the spirit whispered to them as they asked kneeling.
Line upon line, precept upon precept,
They went from Grace to Grace
Until they finally, won the race!

Only the truly penitent are saved.
Alma 42:24

—⁓⤳⟊⟊⟊⟊⟊⤳⁓—

Oh My

Oh how I love Jesus!
Oh how he loves me!
Of this I wish that the whole world could see!
So that they also could come to be!
As happily loved just as me!
How High are the ways that he teaches to me!
How bright and glorious will my light be!
When I am living in Heaven finally!

Because Jesus walked such a long, lonely path
utterly alone, we do not have to do so.
Jeffrey R Holland

—⁓⤳⟊⟊⟊⟊⟊⤳⁓—

Me

Once upon a time
On a planet far away,
A spirit child was born.
Destined to be a warrior
He was raised up by The Father
To develop all his talents
So he could one day rule.
He toiled and he strived,
He laughed and he cried,
Untill that fateful day
When he found Jesus's side.
He was shown the way
And set on course,
To become all that he could,
One day a God.
He laboured all day
To learn the ways of Love,
The ways mastered by the Gods above.
And waited anxiously to hear them say,
Come little child
Right this way.

It is not how you start the race or where you are during the
race, it is how you cross the finish line that will matter.
Robert D. Hales

Oh Jesus!

I want to be who you want me to be,
So the world can see just how happy
By having a Christ like countenance one can be!
Such intelligence doth you teach to me!
Oh how I wish that I could share,
But there are so many that just don't care.
They see the gospel as plain and without flare.
If only they knew someone like you
I am sure that their minds would change.
So please teach me how to be like you
So I can more effectively do this for you!

For us to develop Christlike attributes, we must learn
about the Saviour and follow in his ways.
Mary N Cook

Battle

My trials will I conquer!
My mountains I will crush!
When I get to heaven
I will say:
"Oh what a rush!"
Lord thank you for sending me,
Into mortality!
So that I could learn

And grow to be,
A God just like Jesus!
And a God just like you!
So that I may
One day with you rule!

You need an endowment, in order that you may be
prepared and able to overcome all things
Joseph Smith

———⸙⸙⸙———

Admiral Nick!

Admiral to Gods Armies
That is me!
Look out Satan
You better flee!
For the Lord is teaching me to conquer all!
Look out Satan
Your in for a further fall!
Girded by truths of Eternal natures,
I will follow in the foot steps of my Saviour!
Loyal to the end forever more!
All I can feel is the Love which he pours!
The time is nigh to set things right,
To build up Zion and learn the laws.
And reap the blessings that from Heaven will pour!

I testify that with Christ darkness cannot succeed
Deiter F. Uchtdorf.

In A Blessing To Me

From Grace to Grace
I will grow!
Just like the saviour!
I will be!
To be Exalted on high!
This is my Destiny!
As promised to me!
In a Priesthood blessing
Given to me!
Thank you Father
For Loving me!
Thank you Brother
For teaching me!
All the things I need to learn!
To be in thine presence
Of this I yearn!

His Grace helps us become our best selves.
Dieter F Uchtdorf

Exaltation

I will go
From Grace to Grace
Until that day
That I see your face.
To receive of your fullness
Is what I hope,
To have a fullness of Joy
And Eternal Life,
And to be able to share it all
With my wives!

Your wife is your equal! In marriage neither partner is
superior now inferior to the other. You walk side by side
as a son and daughter of God. She is not to be demeaned
or insulted but should be respected and loved.
Thomas S Monson

Tell Me Why?

How I pray
Not to stray,
Off the path
Here I wish to stay.
For I feel,
A Love so real,
I now know that there is
No better deal.

Eternal life
With my wives,
Tell me why,
I would choose sin?
Instead of the Eternal Prize
That I wish to win!

God never loses sight of our Eternal potential even when we do.
Carole Stephens

———⟋⟍∘⟋⟍∘⟋⟍⟋⟍∘∘⟍⟍———

Why

What can I do for thee?
Thou knowest all things
What can I do for thee?
Thou created all things
What can I do for thee?
Thou can doest all things
Therefore what need have ye of me?
Yet thou lovest me endlessly,
Oh tell me,
What can I do for thee?

There is no greater joy in life than being anxiously
engaged in the service of the Lord.
M Russell Ballard

———⟋⟍∘⟋⟍∘⟋⟍⟋⟍∘∘⟍⟍———

What Is To Be

What is to be my Lord?
What is the fate that doth await?

Better get some sleep my son,
For the battle is yet to be won.
Gather your strength and align with my will,
So the fullness of joy you may feel.
Greatness awaits you in the days to come,
Something unimaginable for the darkness you will not succumb.
Continue to seek and you shall find,
The treasures that await you at the end of time.

As one of his special witnesses, I testify that the outcome of this battle
that began in the premortal life is not in question. Lucifer will lose.
Boyd K Packer

Oh My Lord

Your eyes are like a wild blazing fire
I dare not look into.
In them I can see such Power
That I have never before beheld.
It causes me to tremble
With an awe I have not known.
Oh how I yearn for the day
When you will call me one of your own.

You will one day stand aside and look at your difficult times
and you will realise that he was always there beside you.
Thomas S Monson

———～ഗᏑᏋᏚᏋᏚᏋᏚᏋᏚᏎᎧᏍ～———

The Third Heaven

What is it like to live there?
What is there to do?
Someday I hope to live there
And with all of my wives too!

Salvation is an individual matter, but exaltation is a family matter.
Dallin H Oaks

———～ഗᏑᏋᏚᏋᏚᏋᏚᏋᏚᏎᎧᏍ～———

Oh What A Friend

Oh what a friend is knowledge to me,
Oh how my eyes are beginning to see,
All the horrors of this world,
Needlessly caused by iniquity.
Oh what a friend is he to me,
Sent from heaven straight to me.
Accompanied by love from above,
Oh what a friend is knowledge to me.

As the scales fall of my eyes,
Heaven onward doth I fly.
Oh what a friend is knowledge to me,
Every night he makes me cry,
Out of Love but often sorrow,
During these reverent times,
Comfort from Heaven doth I borrow.
Oh what a friend is knowledge to me.

The best way to obtain truth and wisdom is not to ask from
books, but to go to God in prayer, and obtain divine teaching.
Joseph Smith

Even I

Temptations loose their power when thou art nigh,
You help me to conquer all my trials when I try.
So grateful I am you can tell when I cry,
For I know you are watching,
Even lowly I.

Perhaps at no other time do we feel the divine love of the
saviour as abundantly as we do when we repent.
Linda S Reeves

The Tree Of Life

Oh how happy the man
Who partakes of that tree,
Oh how filled that that man
His joy can be,
Oh how wonderful to know
Gods Eternal mysteries,
Oh how wonderful to learn
How to escape that misery.
What an amazement
To understand
He who loves,
And comprehends,
All my troubles
And all my sorrows,
To him,
I will forever follow,
Forever I will dwell
In his presence and glory,
Forever and ever,
This is my story!

Though you may feel that no one can understand the depth
of your despair, our Saviour, Jesus Christ, understands.
Dieter F Uchtdorf

If There

If there was but one desire what would it be?
If there was but one person who would it be?
If there was but one Heart how would it feel?
If there was but one mind what would it think?
If there was but one will what would it do?
If there was but one time when would it be?
If there was but one life what would you do?

We should look to and have our focus firmly fixed
upon the Saviour at all times and in all places.
David A Bednar

—⁓⁓⁓⁓⁓⁓⁓⁓—

I Hope To Inspire

It is for the wellbeing of your soul that I seek
That you may search for the wonders of Eternity!
Hopefully inspired through my poetry
To search for the wonders of Eternity!
For there are many, there are more than a few,
Can you imagine an endless existence?
Your mortal time is but a test,
To determine how you will spend the rest,
Of Eternity coupled in immortality.
And if you pass, you will earn,
Kingdoms, Dominions and Endless Glory!
So how would you like this to be at the end of your mortality?

So come my friends and learn of Gods Glory!
That you yourself may learn to be Holy,
So that at the end of time
You will win,
The Eternal Prize because you conquered sin!

Because we are Eternal beings, endings are merely interruptions,
a temporary pause in our Eternal progression, which will
one day seem small in the Eternal Joy waiting for us.
Deiter F Uchtdorf

Songs For Zion

The spirits of men were not equal. They may have had an equal start, and we know they were all innocent in the beginning; but the right of free agency which was given to them enabled some to outstrip others
Joseph F Smith Jr

How will you use your agency?

—⁓ꙮ⁓—

A Heavenly Mother

O my preciousness I wish you well,
As you embark on your journey through that living hell.
Know that we will be watching you,
And doing our best to help you in all that you do.
Remember that we will respect the choices you make,
But if you wish to return to us you must learn our ways.
I wish you the best and I pray you will find,
The straight and narrow way,
That leads to a life like mine.

Our theology begins with Heavenly Parents. Our
highest aspiration is to be like them.
Dallin H Oaks

A Heavenly Father

Oh my children look at you all!
I wish that you all could see!
All of the wonders that I have in store!
For you in Eternity!
But for the ones who are proven true!
How more blessed they will be!
For everything that I have will be theirs!
If they will only promise me!
That they will keep my commandments!
And strive to be!

Of one Heart and mind with me!
My Spirit I will send to guide the way!
All you have to do is turn your every thought unto me!

Look unto me in every thought; doubt not, fear not.
D&C 6:36

———∿∿∘⊂⦿⊃∘∿∿———

Our Older Brother The Saviour

Oh no! What have you done!
You've accumulated a debt you cannot pay!
Heavenly Father please send me!
For I can see no other way!
If I don't go they will be lost!
And they will all be gone away!
I understand all that I will have to endure!
But I love my brethren so much!
Send Me Father! I will go!
And show to them the way!
That if they choose to follow!
They may live with thee again!

We rejoice in all the Saviour has done for us. He has made it
possible for each of us to gain our salvation and exaltation.
Quentin L Cook

———∿∿∘⊂⦿⊃∘∿∿———

The Truly Penitent

Who can rejoice too much in the Lord!
From whom the river of mercy rains!
I cannot say the smallest part!
Of that which I now feel!
He rescued my Soul from the deepest pain!
He withheld the sword of Justice!
Sentencing me not to an Eternal despair!
He clenched me with his Love!
And showed to me the ways above!
Teaches to me the ways to salvation!
Now my brethren can Ye harken!
What natural man is there?
That knoweth these things?
None!
Only the truly penitent can sing this song!

Alma 26

The Loving Husband

Ah my Wife! You are my Life!
Without you life would not be the same!
You are the spice that adds to life!
It's wonderful tastes!!
The smell of your beauty!
And the taste of your scent!

Is what makes my life magnificent!
So with all my heart!
I have you to thank!

Let husband and wife never speak to one another
in loud tones unless the house is on fire.
David O Mckay

The Loving Wife

Oh my King! My bells you ring!
As to me your heart sings!
I love you my dear! I always will!
You are my well of serene!
Can you see the gleam in my eye!
You cause me with happiness to cry!
At night when you sleep!
I gaze at you!
And pray that you will always love me too!

Choose your love, love your choice.
Thomas S Monson

The Priest

Ah my wife! Let me show you!
Just how much Heavenly Father loves you!
Through my eyes! I hope you can see!
This love that is in me! He gave to me!
I hope that I can show you throughout our life!
A taste of Heaven for being my wife!
I hope and pray that you can see!
Just how much I do appreciate thee!
I hope and pray that I am worthy!
To receive Fathers counsel!
On how to lead thee!
And that together we may raise!
A righteous posterity!
And that we may be!
Exalted together for Eternity!

Sandwiched between their once upon a time and happily
ever after they all had to experience great adversity.
Dieter F Uchtdorf

———〜〰〜〜〜〜〜〰〜———

The Priestess

Oh my Priest! How is it that!
You can hear! Heavenly Father talk back!
What does he say? How does he sound?
And doth he speak with a smile or a frown?

Where does he live? What does he do?
Did the answer to this he leave any clues?
How is it that he always knows what to do?
And why is it that he reveals it to you?
Thank you my Priest! Thank you my King!
For living your life worthily!
That this song I may sing!

Prayer is so essential a part of revelation that without it
the veil may remain closed to you. Learn to pray, pray
often, prayer is your personal key to heaven.
Boyd K Packer

The Philosopher Kings

They love wisdom!
They love to learn!
Improvement and progression,
Of this they yearn!
What is my ignorance!
What is stopping me!
From improving and progressing,
This gives my life its meaning.
Don't forget to take everything you read
To the Holy Ghost for polishing and cleaning!

The Gospel embrace all correct philosophies, by asking Mr
Holy Ghost you will know which ones are correct!

The Journey

Oh what joy the journey holds
For he, whom to follow Jesus, chose.
Such treasure along the way
Will he find everyday!
There are endless lessons to learn!
The answers he can know
By asking God himself,
And turning unto him, your every thought,
To which you will receive, a stupor of thought
If it be, a thing of naught.
But if it be right, then you surely will,
In your bosom, you will feel.
A mighty burning from within,
Giving you cause to thank,
Great and Mighty him.

If any of you lack wisdom let him ask of God that
giveth to all men liberally and upbraideth not!
James 1:5

The Wise Virgin

She loves her husband with all her Heart,
And would never ask him from his God to part.
Seeks understanding from the Spirit within,
That she may become one with him.
Slow to anger, and quick to forgive,
She seeks to serve others for as long as she lives.
With her heart she loves her God,
And truly lives the ways of the Rod.
She seeks to do all that he requires,
And is daily refined in the refiners fire.
She is wise in all her ways,
And spends her days wisely,
Learning all of his ways.
Of her talents she multiplies,
And of her tongue, never a lie.
Oh my goodness this woman doth make my heart cry.

Each act of dedication and obedience is a drop added to our store.
Spencer W Kimball

———

The Foolish Virgin

The foolish Virgin taketh many forms,
She has a lamp but carries no oil.
Foolish is she in all her ways,
But blinded to her foolishness

You can tell by her gaze.
She goes to church, but knows not the doctrine.
"I know the church is true!" You will hear her say,
But she prepareth herself not for that Great and dreadful day.
Quick to anger and slow to forgive,
A grudge she will hold for as long as you live.
Often a time, she will ignore you,
Or smile at you and ask how do you do.
But her words are like oil that from her mouth spew.
She means them not with a sincere desire,
For her heart is filled with rage and hell fire.
When your back is turned she will speak of you,
Unkind words and find fault continuously with you.
Of her own flaws she is unaware,
For she pleads not with God to strip her bare.

The oil of conversion can not be borrowed
from the lamp of testimony.
David Bednar

One Day We Will Be Together Again

When I pass through the veil
I know I will see you again!
For the spirit testifies
These truths to me.
That one day we will be,
Together again!

Happily again!
One big, Eternal, Family!
We were sealed in the temple
The House of the Lord.
Forever together we will be!
A family again!
Till then my friend,
I will miss you every day.
Until again when I will see you again.
Coupled with Eternal Glory.
Forever to spend,
All my days by your side,
Together a family!
Happy as can be
In the presence of God,
With you I hope to be!
So be patient my friend,
For One day we will stand.
Together at the foot,
Of our family tree!

While we are mourning the loss of our friend, others
are rejoicing to meet him behind the veil.
John Taylor

Rewards

Let the pauper eat, drink and be merry.
Let the wise man seek wisdom and God's Glory.

Let truth and knowledge be the treasure of Kings,
That the hearts of their people they may win.
Let exaltation be the prize for he,
Who works diligently to conquer sin.
That he may seek his reward expectantly,
And that it will not be taken from him.

Exaltation is our goal, discipleship is our journey.
Dieter F Uchtdorf

Priceless

I once asked God to send me a diamond,
I closed my eyes and then looked around.
You'll never guess what i then found.
I saw a lump of coal,
Sitting before me, upon the ground.
I broke it to pieces hoping to find,
A priceless gem that I could call mine.
But to no avail, there was not even a dime.
A few weeks later God sent to me,
A missionary to kindly tell me.
That if I were patient and applied extreme pressure,
That lump of coal, a diamond would one day hold.
The spirit impressed upon me, the depth of this story,
That I was the coal, and that if I was too be patient,
And endure the pressure well,
I would be the gem the most desirable of all!

A diamond was once just a piece of coal
that endured the pressure well!

This Is Just The Beginning!

This is just the beginning!
There will be no end!
For those brave enough!
To follow Heavenly Fathers plan!
Can you do it?
Will you try?
Crowns and Kingdoms!
Dominions and Glory!
My my my, my friends!
This is only the beginning of the Story!
See it goes on forever for those who stay true!
An Endless posterity for me! And you?

Love is intended to last longer than time, to span
the veil of death and continue everlastingly.
Robert L Millet

The Game Of Mortality

Repentance means change!
This is the game!
Do you want to play?
It's a co-operative game!
There can be infinite winners!
There needs be no losers!
All you have to do is to learn all the rules,
And then pray to God to show you what to do!
Just try your best and then rely on him,
And don't forget the most important of all,
To take every thought, unto him!
You will become better and better!
And even more beautiful than before!
By adhering to the commandments,
For this is exactly what they are for!
To make you fit to inherit your royal heritage!
As Kings and Queens to a divine Godship!
If you get stuck or don't know the way,
Simply remember,
All you have to do is study and pray!
Good luck!!!

Look unto me in every thought
D&C 6:36

The Humble Seeker Of Happiness

The wisest man alive is the humble seeker of happiness,
He seeks after a treasure that cannot be bought,
It is a prize that over many wars are fought.
To have this gift, men give their lives,
In order to keep it, many are willing to die.
But greater is there than the happiness of man,
That which I speak of is God's great plan.
His teachings enable us to learn of a happiness divine,
That which God enjoys yea a love so fine.
Kings would give up all that they had,
If they knew the joy that God has.
He who has tasted of it cannot forget,
It will be all that now fills his head.
How do I get more?
How do I keep it?
Please God teach me, how do I receive it?

Master the commandments Son that's what they are for,
And not just some, but learn them all.
My Spirit I will send to teach you how,
If you would only ask me now.
The more you apply the happier you will be,
Come on and try me and you will see!

Happiness is the objective of our Existence!
Joseph Smith

———⚬⚬⚬⚬⚬———

Happy Little Mormons

We're happy little Mormons as happy as happy can be!
We say our grace daily before breakfast, lunch and tea!
Our mummies say where growing closer
to Heavenly Father every day!
He gave the Spirit to us to lead and guide the way!
Because we love our Saviour like,
Yes we all adore our Saviour like,
We're happy as can be!

True happiness come only from making others happy!
David O Mckay

The Apprentice Of God

Of all the jobs this world has to offer,
This man has chosen the Greatest of all!
He is truly ambitious for there is nothing Greater,
Then to learn from God, the Greatest of all!
You best apply sooner, because after this life,
There is no later.
All that is required to apply for this role,
Is willingness and obedience, and to you God will show,
He will magnify your capabilities as you
prove to him your dependability,
He will help you to do this as you show to him your availability.
It is not as easy to others as it is some,

It just truly depends on what your heart wants.
Do you want the honour and glory of man and this world,
Or can you see through the chains and the darkness in disguise?
If your heart has trouble in deciding what it wants,
Simply pray to your Father to help you to choose a side.

God does not begin by asking us about our ability but
only about our availability, and if we then prove our
dependability, he will increase our capability.
Neal A Maxwell

The Rock Of Togetherness

If a marriage is to stand the test of time and all Eternity,
It must be built upon a rock,
Least the storm should come and down it knock.
The Holy Ghost must be your guiding star,
To aid your journey's near and far.
Closer and closer you will grow,
As to the Iron Rod you both hold.
All his commandments you must find
And learn them all before the end of time.
Pray together and think for what for,
Even if it is for money and how to get more.
Believe me when I tell you this,
If you are worthy and it be his will,
So many blessings to you he will pour,
He will open all the right doors,
Until you are unable to receive any more.

None of us marry perfection, we marry potential.
Robert D Hales

Knock Knock

If you want to find him,
Relentless must you be.
For he hideth in his hiding place,
And very well hidden is he.
It starts with hope that exist he might,
And a prayer in place will demonstrate faith.
Faith is a verb, a doing word,
So what should you do,
If you want to find you know who.
Read the scriptures, study and obey,
Ask for guidance and direction,
And don't forget to pray.
Repent continuously,
And pray unceasingly,
Whilst listening and awaiting the Holy Ghost,
For what he has to tell you,
Matters the most.
If you get stuck or need a hand,
Just kneel down and ask
For him to help you understand.
It is of the utmost importance that this you do,
Because where you spend Eternity will depend on you.

Behold, I stand at the door, and knock; if any man

hear my voice, and open the door, I will come in to
him, and will sup with him, and he with me.
Revelations 3:20

The Truly Ambitious

By owning your weaknesses and praying for strengths,
One can grow to be Great and Mighty.
Like the Saviour who surpassed us all,
You too can go from Grace to Grace,
Until you finally conquer all!
Thus receiving the fullness of the Father,
Graduating mortality with flying colours!
What you will learn will be all that matters,
For it will be all that you can take with you
When this temporal world shatters.

Good timber does not grow with ease. The
stronger the wind the stronger the trees.
Thomas S Monson

The Artist Of Self

Everyday he desires to be,
Something greater than yesterday's he.
He searches high, he searches low,
To see just where, he wants to go.
He hopes to create something magnificent,
He hopes to create something beautiful,
But if he wishes to truly succeed,
He better let God paint this masterpiece.
It won't be easy, it will take work,
But pray unceasingly,
And take your thoughts to him continuously,
And you will find, given time,
Just how beautiful, is his Heart and mind.

No other choice we make can make of us what he can.
Thomas S Monson

———〰️○⟨⟩○〰️———

The Adventurer

He sails the sea of mortality hoping to find,
The straight and narrow gate while there is still time.
He feels and sees what is right and wrong,
As the Holy Spirit, guides him along.
Repenting, exercising faith, doing good and praying continuously,
And by turning every thought unto God,
He draws nearer to Him incessantly.

He climbs the highest mountains,
And scales the steepest cliffs,
He crosses vast oceans,
And conquers every twist,
By listening to his constant companion, the Holy Ghost.
This man will find what matters the most.

The lighthouse of the Lord beckons to all as we sail the seas of life.
Thomas S Monson

The Wise Man

The wise delight in understanding and knowledge,
While fools will turn their heads and hide their eyes,
Or lash out and try to rationalise.
Justified reproach to the wise is more valuable than silver and gold,
For it is the currency in which upon Eternal life you may hold.
By acknowledging weakness and praying for strengths,
One can grow to be stronger than many many men.
With this might, yea a gift from God,
Power will he have to hold to the rod.

My Grace is sufficient for all men that humble themselves before
me, for if they humble themselves before me, and have faith in
me, then will I make weak things become strong unto them.
Ether 12:27

Just A Glimpse

Just a glimpse has caught my eye!
Of that sphere that dwells so high!
But enough to make me cry,
And make me wish,
I was ready to die.

We are made of the stuff of Eternity. Endings are not our destiny.
Dieter F Uchtdorf

The Scriptures

She is the diamond of my Heart!
She is the gem of my Soul!
She is the pearl of my mind!
She is the treasure of my life!
She has been sent straight from heaven!
To guide me home!

A chapter a day will light your way!

My God

He is the doctor to my Soul.
All my problems doth he know.
Even those matters,
That I never had told.
Even of matters,
That I didn't even know.
All my wounds,
Doth he stitch.
Until not left,
Not even an itch.
Bit by bit,
Little by little.
It sometimes feels,
Not more than a tickle.
Other times though,
This I feel.
A fire within me,
That is so surreal.
Burning away,
All my pain.
As I call upon,
His Mighty Name.

The Atonement leaves, no traces. What it fixes is fixed.
It just heals, and what it heals stays healed.
Boyd K Packer

Agency Is The Freedom To Choose

The Gift of Agency
It is always a choice,
A choice to be good
Or a choice to be bad,
A choice to be happy
Or a choice to be sad,
A choice to be friendly
Or a choice to be mad,
A choice to smile
Or turn it upside down,
But either way
Always remember,
It was your choice to frown.

I have two choices, I can choose to be happy or I
can choose to be sad. I choose to be happy!
Marjorie Pay Hinckley

The Gift of Agency

Agency is a powerful thing
When you learn to control it.
You can choose to say
I forgive you, let's forget it.
Agency is a powerful thing
When you don't control it.

You can choose to say
I hate you and I'll never forget it.
It can cause you to be in bondage
Or to be free in the Heart.
But both stem from the choices
That you made at the start.
Which way you use your agency
Will set you apart.
For good or for evil
Depends on your Heart.
So stop and think
And pray for direction,
For your Heavenly Fathers Guidance,
His love and affection.
To show you the way
the way you should go.
To be able to follow
The straight and narrow.
The one that will lead you
To life Eternal,
The one that will lead you
To a life so supernal.
So pray unceasingly
And as Alma of old,
Promised that you will know
Of mysteries untold.

Your agency, the right to make choices, is not given so that you
can get what you want. This divine gift is provided so that you
will choose what your Father in Heaven wants for you. That
way He can lead you to become all that he intends you to be.
Elder Scott

The Time is Nigh!

Now I raise my fists!
As did Moroni!
As the time to stand is nigh!
To look evil in the eye!
And to sing the Heavenly war cry!
The trumpet will sound!
And the Angels will gather around!
Zion will be found and the temple will be built!
And the Lord will grab, his sword by the hilt!
In a cloud of Glory he will come!
With all of Heavens Armies!
This my friends is the next chapter
In this never ending story!

An inland Empire will be established in these valleys of the
mountains, which will be a place of refuge for millions of people
to gather to when the great day of the judgements of God comes
upon the earth. We will be shut out from the rest of the world.
Brigham Young

My Endowment

Tomorrow I visit the house of God!
What lies ahead of me! O such is a mystery!
Will I see into immortality? Will I see God?
Will I see the tree of life? And the Iron Rod?

Will I feel the Endlessness of Eternity?
And the presence of Gods Glory?
O come tomorrow!
The next chapter of my story!

You need an Endowment, brethren, in order that you
may be prepared and able to Overcome All Things.
Joseph Smith

My Lady The Temple

O the temple what a Queen!
Her majesty and awe make me want to scream!
She is so filled with wonder! I wonder what I will find!
When I enter into the temple, one more time!

Enter this door as if the floor were gold;
And every wall of jewels all of wealth untold;
As if a choir in robes of fire were singing here;
No shout nor rush, but hush, for God is here.
Spencer W Kimball

Lost In The Celestial Room

It seemed to me that time was stilled!
And that this was how Eternity feels!
Excuse me Sir, it's time to go!
The Temple, is now closed!
What! How can that be! I just arrived!
Sir you've been sitting here since I arrived.

In the temple, all feelings of inadequacy
and imperfection begin to fade.
Rosemary M Wixom

The Celestial Room

When I sit there he sits with me!
And I feel like I am living in a dream!
A love so clean envelopes me!
As his gentle words stream to me!

Son thank you for seeking me!
In return I will grant thee this!
My most cherished daughter to be Exalted with!
Thank you Father you know me so well!
For this is my Greatest desire!
To be sealed to a woman!
As beautiful as thee!
Through all of time!
And for all Eternity!

This house and others like it become the bridge between
this life and the Eternal life that lies beyond.
Gordon B Hinckley

The Celestial Room 2

It feels so clean!
And everything gleams!
A thousand rainbows light the sky!
And the air is laced with ecstasy!
The light seems to from Heaven shine!
With a Golden glow! No matter the time!
The Greatest treasures are hidden from sight!
But if you feel and see! I Guarantee!
You will find yourself! Living your wildest dreams!
It feels like a place birthed in the realms of fantasy!
But instead this is the door way to my destiny!
The beginning of a new journey!
The Gateway to Gods Glory!
The next episode of my story!

It is in the temple that we remember who we really are
and see with clarity who we really can become.
Jean A Stevens

In The Temple

O precious serenity, I wish to wed thee.
Thou must be a woman because thou art to die for.
Where have you been all my life?
How is it that I just met you.
I wish for us to never part,
For your presence is of the most desirable of arts.

I think there is no place in the world where I feel closer
to the Lord than in one of his holy temples.
Thomas S Monson

The Key To Our Soul

The knowledge of the Gospel is the key to our Souls.
Study it hard and listen to the Spirit
For he will tell you the way in which you should grow!
So much wisdom he will teach
Such intelligence that you were never before told.
Absorb all that they bestow,
And of their words you should learn to know.
That you might not, just grow old,
But grow unto perfection as God once did,
Who now on High on his Throne sits.
Till we all come in the unity of the faith,
And of the knowledge of the Son of God,
Unto a perfect man,
Unto the measure of the stature of the fullness of Christ.

And he gave some, apostles; and some, prophets; and
some, evangelists; and some, pastors and teachers.
For the perfecting of the saints, for the work of the
ministry, for the edifying of the body of Christ
Till we all come in the unity of the faith, and of the
knowledge of the Son of God, unto a perfect man, unto
the measure of the stature of the fulness of Christ
Ephesians 4:11-13

Endure Well

Please me humble, please be meek.
This is pure strength, it is in no ways weak.
If you are able to endure the heat well,
Practicing patience while you stroll through hell.
Pleading for Grace to aid and strengthen,
Praying for guidance to make those corrections.
Listening anxiously for that still small voice,
As you turn unto God, your every thought.
You will one day master them all,
That which is plain and precious, above them all.
Your calling and election you will hear made sure,
By a visit from his majesty, our Lord and Saviour.

Small efforts sustained over time can produce significant results.
Devin G Durrant

The Key To Our Soul 2

Such a treasure is knowledge to me,
To my Soul it is the key.
Held by God with it he sets me free,
As he slowly unlocks me.
All my walls he is tearing down,
One by one they all fall down.
With gentle persuasion and words of wisdom,
He teaches me to understand all with patience.
Shines his light down on me,
And causes the darkness within to flee.
Slowly and steadily this mountain I climb,
This one I must conquer before the end of time.

One drop at a time!
Russel Ballard

―――✺―――

Every Thought

When you turn your Heart to God,
Yea even unto your every thought.
He will teach you a new point of view,
One that which you before never knew.
You only need to follow the trail of clues,
Left by God, through his chosen few.
If everyday, this you do,
Study and ponder upon each clue.
I guarantee, this you will find,

A story that will be, similar to mine.
A change of Heart so mighty,
It will cause you to cry.
Oh my God!
For my sins did you die!
Thank you for what you did!
Of my heart,
You have won the bid!

Turn unto me your every thought
D&C 6:36

Seek Ye First The Kingdom Of God

Can you put first your search for him?
Can you seek him above all?
Above worldly treasures, family and friends?
Can you to his needs attend?
Would you leave it all behind?
If the pearl of great price, you came to find?
Will you give to him your all?
Might, mind, strength, heart and all?
Will you for his cause stand tall?
No matter how the world tries to make you feel small?
Will you seek for the treasures of eternity?
Even when people say you have lost your sanity?
Could you stand against the crowd?
Even if they threatened to kick you out?

What would you do if they conspired against you?
To commit evil and even kill you?

No good thing comes without effort and sacrifice.
Dieter F Uchtdorf

———⟨ornament⟩———

How Far?

How far would you go to find him?
Would you turn the TV off to look for him?
Would you listen to the radio or sing a hymn?
Would you go out with your friends,
Or stay home to learn from him?
Sunday is easy, everybody does that,
What about Monday to Saturday,
What do you call that?
Do you listen to the whisperings from within?
Or has it given up because you weren't listening?
Do you doubt not and fear not?
And turn to him your every thought?
How often do you knock?
And ask if you can come in?
How much time do you really spend,
Looking for him?

God will add his power to his servants efforts.
Henry B Eyring

———⟨ornament⟩———

The Cutest Kids

Oh how they have to be,
The cutest people that I have ever seen!
I cannot believe they think me mean,
I am only trying to help them see!
I love them so much I just want to see,
All of them Exalted here with me!
The promises given to me are sure!
Exaltation is my destiny!
It takes hard work oh please won't you try!
It will be to late after you die!
I will do whatever it takes!
To make you move before it's to late!

Continue with good cheer for your fullness
of joy awaits you in Heaven!
Shayne M Bowen

———∽∿∞∾∿∽———

Do You?

Do you keep all the commandments that he gave?
Or just the law of chastity,
Like the foolish virgins that didn't know he?
Do you carry oil for your lamp?
Or will your flame the world not withstand?
Do you seek to emulate him?
Or are you content just to know of him?

Do you know the depths of his Soul?
Or just of the stories that you have been told?
I don't mean through this poem to scold,
But I just think of this you should know,
That more of him there is to find,
If you are only willing to take the time.

Be of good cheer! The future is as bright as your faith!
Thomas S Monson

—————⁓ⱳ⌒∘ⱺⱳ⌒⌒⌒∘ⱳ⌒⌒∘ⱳ⌒∘ⱳ—————

Patiently And Persistently

Patiently and persistently this mountain I climb,
Eating the elephant one bite at a time.
Oh how I wonder when I will find,
The top of this mountain that I now climb.

Repentance is a process and not something that happens
at one particular moment. It requires consistency.
Francisco J Vinas

—————⁓ⱳ⌒∘ⱺⱳ⌒⌒⌒∘ⱳ⌒⌒∘ⱳ⌒∘ⱳ—————

Commandments

There are so many,
There are more than a few,
I speak of the commandments,
That God gave you.
If you think that there are only ten,
Well my friend, you best look again!
How about the one on Eternal marriage,
Or how about the commandment to stop finding fault in me,
To be stripped of all pride,
Or God you are not yet ready to see.
Or how about feeding the hungry,
And helping the needy?
For without charity you are a nothing to be.
We are commanded to fight for our freedoms,
To uphold the laws that God gave to us that we may be free.
Or what about becoming perfect, even as he?
Through receiving Grace, and to feel and see?
Surmounting all our challenges, not to just endure,
But to come off conqueror, above them all!
To pray always, without ceasing,
Crying always, with your heart bleeding,
To the Lord, to whom you should pour.
Sincerely repenting,
And working out your salvation, even unto fear and trembling.
Or the one how not to grumble, and how we are to remain humble.
If you want the prize to win,
I suggest you look again,
Simply because,
No unclean thing,
Can enter in.
And in ignorance you cannot,
Be saved within.

It is impossible for a man to be saved in ignorance.
D&C 131:6

Fulfil Your Potential

We are here to become one with God,
To inherit all that he has!
And to the royal Kingdom,
One day to be Heirs.
This does not only include
Only that of a physical nature,
But one mind and one heart,
Requires there be nothing apart.
You have the potential,
To be just like him,
Should you choose to follow,
The path free from sin.
Through forgiveness and repentance,
Each and every day,
Line upon line,
Precept upon precept,
You will begin to hear him say,
The things you need to correct,
And grace he will provide to you,
To strengthen, change, redeem and renew.
But only after you try to do,
All that you can do.
Of this my friends,
I make this promise to you.

Line upon line and precept upon precept, gradually and almost
imperceptibly, our motives, our thoughts, our words, and
our deeds become aligned with the will of God. Conversion
unto the Lord requires both persistence and patience.
David A Bednar

Help Me!

Help Me!
Teach Me!
Please don't leave Me!
I need you every hour!
I need your mighty Power!
For the night doth draw near
And I haven't yet mastered all that is dear!
Please dear God, bestow upon me thine Grace.
So that a chance I may have, to win this race.
That I may behold thy beautiful face.
I cannot do it on my own!
For how am I to learn of things unknown?
Unless you teach me, I will get lost!
And the price to pay comes at too high a cost.
So please give me thine spirit so that I may discern,
And that the Eternal reward I might earn.

Being the literal premortal children of the Father, you and I can,
by going from Grace to Grace, eventually receive the fulness of
the Father as Jesus did. In addition to being resurrected we can
become perfect, or in one set of meanings from the greek, finished,

completed and fully developed. But only if we worship (love) God
and Truly follow the example of our redeemer Jesus Christ. After
all Brothers and Sisters, the ultimate adoration is emulation.
Neil A Maxwell

The Process Of Repentance

The process of repentance,
Is not a prison sentence.
But rather a gift, designed to lift,
The soul, to greater heights untold!
Higher and higher you will sore,
Life will become anything but a bore!
You will grow and come to adore,
The God who helped you overcome all.

True repentance is about transformation, not torture or torment.
Dieter F Uchtdorf

So Many

How do I follow, how do I obey?
There are so many commandments,
That to me God gave.

It seems impossible, that I could learn,
Everything that he asks, so that the reward I can earn.

I would not command you, least I prepared a way,
That you could keep my commandments, in every way.
The Holy Ghost I have sent you, to be by your side.
To guide you, lead you and teach you as you continuously strive.
My Son I sent to die for you, so that Grace could be unlocked.
That he could provide succour to you, when you know not.
I told you to try your hardest, and to feel and to see.
That you might know what the commandments, mean to me.

I will go and do the things which the Lord hath commanded,
for I know that the Lord giveth no commandments unto the
children of men, save he shall prepare a way for them that they
may accomplish the thing which he commanders them.
1 Nephi 3:7

Listen

Listen carefully and listen closely and you will hear,
The still small voice whispering in your ear.
He will tell you what to do,
And you will hear that God loves you.

God loves you this very day and always.
Dieter F Uchtdorf

Ask For A Hand

If you don't understand,
Any of God's commands.
It's ok!
He will give you a hand!
He will teach you how he wants them followed.
Let him lead you to the straight and narrow.
You can guess and even pretend,
But unless you ask for his helping hand.
The road you follow will be your own.
Giving you reason,
On that Great day to moan.
So turn unto him your every thought.
And praise your God for your soul he hath bought.
That you might have this wonderful opportunity
To learn the ways above and to prove yourself worthy.
If you don't, you will be dammed.
Destined to spend Eternity
Shouting curses at this missed opportunity.

"Now, it may be contended that a judgment, with some degree of salvation for all, encourages the sinner to pursue his dark ways. Not so. However generous the judgment, it is measured by our works. Our punishment will be the heavy regret that we might have received a greater reward, a higher kingdom, had our lives conformed more nearly to truth. Such remorse may yield keener pain than physical torture." (Understandable Religion, p. 89)
John Widtsoe

One With God

What could be better than to become one with God?
To share his mind even unto every thought.
How Great would it be to think like he,
Who possesses all knowledge and all the keys.
All wisdom does he know and you will also,
When you become one with God.

And the Lord called his people Zion, because they
were of one heart and one mind, and dwelt in
righteousness; and there was no poor among them.
Moses 7:18

Dancing In The Dark

Faith is like dancing in the dark!
When you cannot see a thing!
And you even close your eyes!
Because you trust your partner!
Because he is your Heavenly Father!
And you know all he wants!
Is your Happily Ever After!

For we walk by faith, not by sight.
2 Corinthinans 5:7

At Least I Have God

When the whirlwinds come,
At least I have God.
When people are mean,
At least I have God.
When my trials seem like torture,
At least I have God.
When I have nothing else,
I realise that God is all I need.

No pain that we suffer, no trial that we experience is wasted.
Orson F Whitney

Unforgiveness

How hot the coal of unforgiveness,
It burns its bearer right to the soul.
How bitter to taste, you probably already know,
So before it gets too late, you better let go.
Oh how hot the coal of unforgiveness,
It burns its bearer right to the soul.

I, the Lord will forgive whom I will forgive, but
of you it is required to forgive all men.
D&C 64:10

Who Gets Burnt From Being Unforgiving?

Pity the person who holds onto the coal,
That was picked from the fire so long ago.
For the person who lit it most probably doesn't know,
That in your hand, it's embers still glow.

Sometimes, of all the people in the world, the one who is the
hardest to forgive - as well as perhaps the one who is most in need
of our forgiveness - is the person looking back at us in the mirror.
Dieter F Uchtdorf

Timing

I am trusting in his timing,
This is what having faith includes.
For my father knows best,
This is what I conclude.

Faith in God includes faith in his timing.
Neal A Maxwell

The Bondage Of Being Unforgiving

It will consume your soul to a darkness untold,
Make no mistake it is bitter to taste.
It will deliver you into bondage to that devil of old,
Make no mistake it is bitter to taste.
It will occupy your mind day after day,
Make no mistake it is bitter to taste.
It will cost you your sanity and every thing else,
Make no mistake it is bitter to taste.
It will destroy the child that once dwelt within,
Make no mistake it is bitter to taste.
It will cost you your loved ones,
Make no mistake it is bitter to taste.
It will keep you angry and its flames will consume you,
Make no mistake it is bitter to taste.
You can't be happy while being angry,
So the fullness of joy you will never know,
Make no mistake it is bitter to taste.

Heaven is filled with those who have this in common:
They are forgiven and they forgive.
Dieter F Uchtdorf

The Miracle Of Forgiveness

It will set you free and leave your mind at ease,
After you taste it you will never regret it.
It will unshackle the chains that kept you in pain,
After you taste it you will never regret it.
Make no mistake its fruits are sweet to taste,
After you taste it you will never regret it.
It will heal your wounds and extinguish the flames,
After you taste it you will never regret it.
It will leave you in peace instead of in pieces,
After you taste it you will never regret it.
It will tame the beast that dwells within,
After you taste it you will never regret it.
It will win the battle that is fought within,
After you taste it you will never regret it.
The miracle of forgiveness is simply divine,
I hope that this my friends you can find,
And quickly too before you run out of time.

Somehow forgiveness with love and tolerance accomplishes
miracles that can happen in no other way.
Gordon B Hinckley

Safe And Sound

You will never walk alone after knocking on his door,
For happy is he and he takes it not as a chore.

He delights and rejoices when we seek after him,
He will fight for and teach you to be just like him,
As his greatest desire is to let you in,
But he respects your agency
So it is up to you!
So come quickly my friends come and try him.
Believe in his grace, it's power knows no bounds,
And believe in his timing for it is safe and sound.

Our Father will not force us to love him or to follow
his Son. Our agency is far too important to him.
Sheri Dew

The Enemy

There is a battle going on
And it is for your soul.
It is fought not with guns and bullets
But with a trickiness untold.
The devil and his angels are cunning and crafty,
They seek your destruction and like to play dirty.
Be not light minded for my words are true,
They are very sneaky and they desire for you,
Misery and heartache, sadness and doom
Always a near, they constantly loom,
Lurking in their hiding place they do await,
Seeking to deter you from entering that Gate.

His favourite trick is to pretend to be your friend,

earn your trust, and then lead you away slowly but
steadily, line upon line, precept upon precept.

Gods Love

People come and people go,
But my God will never leave me alone.
For he loves me with a love I have not known,
A love that seems, to just grow and grow.
In so many ways does his love show,
I cannot tell you, yet this you must know.

It is the Greatest thing.

How Do You Love God?

How do you love a God that you do not know?
How do you love a God that you have never met?
How do you love a God from stories you hear told?
How do you love a God that you once knew so long ago?
Through his spirit!
Sent from on High to guide you by,
It will teach you of a love so high.
It is not pushy, it is not a drag,

It will never whine or nag.
It will show you what love is,
Then you may return it to whose rightfully it is.

He is simply unlike anybody you know.

The Deadly Fog Of Pride

Blinding us we cannot see,
The road to follow that would set us free.
The fog of pride covers our eyes,
And in our heart it occupies.
Curseth the deadly fog of pride.

A lack of absence of humility or teachableness. Pride sets
people in opposition to each other and to God. A proud person
sets himself above those around him and follows his own
will rather than God's will. Conceit, envy, hardheartedness,
and haughtiness are also typical of a proud person
Lds.org

The Battle

Everyday the war is fought,
As we battle to practice that which we are taught!
To choose the right, we must constantly fight!
In this our Father takes delight!
To see us grow and emulate Jesus,
The only begotten sent here to save us!

If we are on the right path it will always be uphill.
Henry B Eyring

Devils

Devils do act upon us each and everyday.
Unaware we are of in just how many ways.
They cause us to contend with each other,
Get angry and disobey.
Devils do act upon us each and everyday.
Turn all your Heart, mind, strength and might!
To your God that he may teach you how to fight.
That one day you just may,
Learn of all the devils evil ways.
That you may come of conquerer,
And posses your own Soul.
That you may master yourself,
And learn to be in control.
Then when you have done this,

You will have reason to sing,
The same song as Alma,
Of a Love Redeeming.

Pray always, that you may come off conqueror; yea, that
you may conquer Satan, and that you may escape the hands
of the servants of Satan that do uphold his work.
D&C10:5

———⟊⟊⟊ᴏᴇ⟊ᴏⓒᴛ⟊ᴏᴏⱳⱳ———

Overwhelmed

The fate of the world keeps me up all night,
The darkness seems to be overwhelming the light.
People now see evil as good,
Whilst many more see good as evil.
Devils singing melodious songs,
Whilst children nod their heads and sing along.

We cannot improve the world if we are conformed to the world.
Neal A Maxwell

———⟊⟊⟊ᴏᴇ⟊ᴏⓒᴛ⟊ᴏᴏⱳⱳ———

My Dearest

Dearest Father, dearest Mother,
Thank you for loving me with a love I've not known,
Thank you for giving me this sweet taste of home.
I love to remember all that you do,
I love to dream about what it would be like with you.
Happy tears fill my heart as you tell me why,
The wise and glorious reasons that we had to say goodbye.
Now hope paves the way as the spirit guides me closer,
To that Great and dreadful day where I will see you again.

I simply cannot wait!

—————

Sometimes

Sometimes I get down and wonder why,
Why is it that I feel so glum.
But then I hear him say to me:

"Let me teach you how to be,
I can show you what it's like,
To be a God, please don't fight.
I can show you of a love so high,
That men would give their lives to try.
So will you come and follow me?"

"Oh yes dear God! Please!
Show me!"

Submission of one's will is really the only uniquely
personal thing we have to place on God's altar.
Neal A Maxwell

When You Finally Meet

Through the portals of immortality the Heart can travel,
Into the realms of the Gods one can reach,
If only you would allow him, you to teach.
Through the whisperings of the still soft voice,
God has given us all a choice.
To listen and obey, or other ways to stray,
The choice is yours, but the rebellious earn no reward.
Whilst the reward for those who pray and seek,
Words cannot describe your reward, when him you finally meet.

Our knowledge of the Saviour, Jesus Christ, and his atonement
helps us to endure our trials and to see purpose in suffering
and to trust God for what we cannot comprehend.
Neal A Maxwell

Mortality

The treacherous trials seem like torture,
But memories of my rejoicing keep me sure,
Of why I came to this Earthly sphere.

You chose this course my son,
You agreed to my plan,
Now buckle up and take my hand.
Follow the guidance that I give to you,
And know and feel that I love you.

It is extremely important for you to believe in yourselves, not only
for what you are now, but for what you have the power to become.
Neal A Maxwell

———∿∾⊙⌀⊙≺⊙⌀∾∿———

What Is God Telling You?

Perhaps the most important thing to do,
Would be to ponder upon these precious clues.
And to feel and see what ye should do.
Once you have learnt and understand,
And Gods character ye comprehend.
God will unfold the Heavens to you,
That which has been hidden
Within these clues,
And mysteries known
Only by a few.

You will feel an urgency to do.
All of that which he hath commanded you.
As you begin to understand,
That which before, you never knew.
Everything that he will unfold to you,
Will aid greatly in strengthening you,
As you realise how of great import,
Are the scriptures and Almighty God.

When we understand the character of God, and know how to come
to him, he begins to unfold the heavens to us, and to tell us all about
it. When we are ready to come to him, he is ready to come to us.
Joseph Smith

———〰◦⌒ɛⱦ◯•ⱷɛ◦◦〰———

The Read But Don't Ask

Perhaps the most common of all,
People read but don't ask God.
Therefore the deeper meaning they will not know,
Of all that God desires to be told.

Ask him! And you will see! A deeper meaning is there to Eternity!

———〰◦⌒ɛⱦ◯•ⱷɛ◦◦〰———

Your Testimony

What can you give away and get back double?
Your testimony.
What can you bear that will always get you out of trouble?
Your testimony.
What will grow and grow but never get old?
Your testimony.
What will save you from the stormy sea?
When it's mighty waves beat upon thee?
Your testimony.
What will lead you to live happily?
Your testimony.
What will eternally strengthen your family?
Your testimony.
What holds the Greatest Reward yet is free?
Your testimony.
What can grow to be as solid as a tree?
That gently sways when pounded by the breeze?
Your testimony.

Seeking for and obtaining a testimony of spiritual
truth requires asking, seeking, and knocking.
David A Bednar

Dear God

Dear God,
Please give me the strength
To conquer this day,
And to overcome anything
That blocks my way.
Give me the strength
That this road I may stay,
That I may be faithful
To thee and not stray.
Teach me to keep thy commandments
And to be worthy to enter the temple.
Teach me to Love
And to be a good example.
That through me others may see,
A Godly Love and the way
That you wish us to be.

We can overcome all of our fears, not all at once, but one
at a time. As we do, so will we grow in confidence
James E Faust

Study The Things Of God

I want to go to the Celestial Kingdom
So I must learn all that I need to do.
I must be sure that I have not missed

Any of these precious clues.
Because one cannot earn the blessings
For that which he did not do.
So I will learn all that there is
And so should you.

And don't forget to ponderize!

———⁓⁓⊙⌇⊙⌇⊙⊙⁓⁓———

What A Precious Thing To Do

What a precious thing to do,
To take a moment each day
To stop and listen
To what the Spirit is trying to say.
To feel and to see,
And To ponder every thought,
To take the time
To ask yourself?
What is he trying to tell me?

We watch, we wait, we listen for that still, small voice.
When it speaks, wise men and women obey!
Thomas S Monson

———⁓⁓⊙⌇⊙⌇⊙⊙⁓⁓———

Who's on the Lords side? Who?

He is Mighty!
He is Strong!
This war I know
Will be won!
It is written in the scriptures!
We cannot loose!
So tell me,
Who's on the Lords side? Who?

The Future of this world has long been declared; the final outcome between good and evil is already Known. There is absolutely no question as to who wins because the victory has already been posted on the scoreboard. The only really strange thing is all of this is that we are still down here on the field trying to decide which team's jersey we want to wear!
Jeffery R Holland

On The Lords Errand

On the Lords Errand
Is where I want to be!
Lord if you have a mission
Won't you please send me!
I will do my best!
I will not rest!

Until I have succeeded!
And thine Errand
I've completed!
I will not weary
Or leave you dismayed,
But for your guidance
I will forever pray!
Until that wonderful moment
On that wonderful day,
When I will be proud to hear you say!
Thy faithful and profitable servant,
Come! Right this way!

No calling in this church is of little or small consequence!

Gordon B. Hinckley

Oh How Blessed Is The Knowledge Of God

How knowledge and understanding
Can make a man happy,
As happy as can be!
To understand the plan more fully
Can bring comfort and joy!
To gain testimonies and understandings
From the spirit of God,
Can dispel your worries
And destroy your fears!

So why not pursue this wonderful journey!
The one that leads into an Eternity,
Of wonders and mysteries!
Of bliss and ecstasy!
And endless adventures
Of magnificent nature's!
There will be planets to explore!
And worlds galore!
To provoke your curiosity!
And expand your mind!
And best of all!
You will never have to worry
About running out of time!

How can we truly understand who we are unless we know
who we were and what we have the power to become? How
can there be real identity without there being real history?
How can one understand his tiny, individual plot without
knowing, even a little, about Fathers grand, galactic plans?
Neal A Maxwell

Requirements

Entrance into the celestial kingdom
Requires more than just mere church attendance.
It requires living the Gospel with absolute diligence.
Patient, kindness, meekness and charity.
Free from lust and contention, chastity and drowning in humility.
Pretending doesn't count, you must be sincere.

To all the commandments you must adhere.
You must experience a change of heart,
Enough to tell you from your old self apart.
Through your gethsemane you must tread.
All your sins you must regret.
As the Saviour you must learn to behave.
And remember,
Only the truly penitent are saved.

Behold, this is joy which none receiveth save it be the
truly penitent and humble seeker of happiness.
Alma 27

Our Daily Bread

Dear God,
I had a rough day.
So I kneel down before thee
And for comfort doth I pray.
That perhaps for a moment,
You could make the pain go away.
But if you think,
It wise to not.
Than perhaps with strength,
You could fill me God.
That I may be able
To endure the heat.
Until the night cometh,
When we finally meet.

The first, the middle, and the last thing to do is pray
Henry B Eyring

Truth Is My Religion

Have you my friends?
Devoted your life,
To the attainment of that
Which the Gods most covert.
That which leads to Life Eternal,
Oh how the possessor
Will enjoy so supernal.
For its nature is ever Eternal.
Throughout the storms
It will travail.
It will be challenged
But to no avail.
Without it you would not know,
The road to follow,
And in circles you would go.
It can be found
On the mountain tops.
Or even in the slums,
Or under a rock.
If you look, feel and see,
The Holy Ghost will tell you if it is he.
With this in mind,
I invite thee.
To fill up your chest,
So that a rich man you will be!

Our religion measures, weighs, and circumscribes all the wisdom
in the world—all that God has ever revealed to man. God
has revealed all the truth that is now in the possession of the
world, whether it be scientific or religious. The whole world are
under obligation to him for what they know and enjoy; they are
indebted to him for it all, and I acknowledge him in all things.
Brigham Young

Is It Truth?

Involve Jesus in your decisions.
Plead with him to teach you reason.
To recognise truth above all,
As the possessor of it will not fall.
Embrace it from wherever you can find it.
For truth is truth no matter who has it.
Take every thought to your God above.
And pray for guidance from his spirit.
.   To whom you should ask,
Is this truth? Is it?

One reason we are on this earth is to discern between
truth and error. This discernment comes through the
Holy Ghost, not just our intellectual faculties.
Ezra Taft Benson

And by the Power of the Holy Ghost ye
may know the truth of all things.
Moroni 10:5

Tell me why?

How I pray
Not to stray,
Off the path
Here I wish to stay.
For I feel,
A Love so real.
I know that there is
No better deal.
Eternal life
With my wives,
Tell me why,
I would choose sin?
Instead of the Eternal Prize
That I wish to win!

We can have Eternal life if we want it, but only
if there is nothing else we want more.
Bruce C Hafen

Help!

Help me!
Teach me!
Please don't leave me!
I need thee every hour!
I need thine mighty power!
For the night doth draw near
And I haven't yet mastered all that is dear.
Please dear God, bestow me thine Grace.
That a chance I may have, to win this race.
That I may behold, thy beautiful face.
I cannot do it on my own.
For how am I to learn of things unknown?
Unless you teach me, I will get lost.
And the price to pay, comes at too high a cost.
So please give me thine spirit, so that I may discern.
That the Eternal reward, I might earn.

Don't you give up. Don't you quit. You keep walking. You keep
trying. There is help and happiness ahead! It will be alright in
the end. Trust God and believe in good things to come.
Jeffrey R Holland

What do I want to be?

If I could be anything what would I be?
Would I be a doctor?

Would I be a pilot?
Would I be a lawyer?
Would I be a judge?
How about president?
Or prime minister?
What I really want to be
Is a loving Heavenly Father to my posterity,
Just as my Father in Heaven is to me!

Your Heavenly Father loves you, each of
you and that love never changes.
Thomas S Monson

What Matters Most

He can give you riches!
He can give you wealth!
But what he wishes for most
Is your Eternal health,
So come and learn,
And you will feel,
His spirit burn
Within you.
To lead you and to guide you
On your way,
He will do this
As you pray.
So say a prayer
Each and everyday,

Heavenly Father
What must I do?
That I may return
To live with you?

Pray to Heavenly Father, listen to the Holy Ghost, follow the
promptings you are given, and all will be well in your life.
Robert D Hales

Joseph

My Faith is unshakable.
My testimony unmistakable.
If a mountain were to fall upon my head,
It would probably mean that I was dead.
But I would still come off conquerer!
For my God, to me, will never forsake.
In him I put forth all of my trust!
For his cause I would rather wear out than rust.
Forever and ever you won't stop me!
Forever and ever I will follow he!

If I were in the deepest cockpit of Nova Scotia, and had
the Rocky Mountains piled on top of me, I would not
be discouraged, and I would come out on top!
Joseph Smith

A Broken Heart And
A Contrite Spirit

Destroyed by the devil,
My soul did he crush.
Led me to do evil,
He reduced me to dust.
Found by the Lord,
He rescued my soul.
And taught me to rise
From the ashes below.
From the deepest pit
He showed me how,
To claw my way out,
Of that endless hell.
Now I will tell you his story.
And I will tell it boldly.
That he lives!
And that he desires to give!
A life so supernal,
And a life of Eternal treasures to he,
He who prayeth unceasingly,
And repenteth continuously.
And if you should find him
Then hooray for you.
And a congratulations
You will hear him tell you.
But until then,
I suggest you read again.
The words of this rhyme,
That in time you may,
Realise that which you may have missed,
So that your heart you may prepare to give.

And ye shall offer for a sacrifice unto me a
broken heart and a contrite spirit.
3 Nephi 9:20

Love & Light

Every piece of knowledge
That comes to Earth.
Proceedeth forth to us
From God above.
He gives to us
The opportune,
To stay poor
Or to amass a great fortune.
It is with our agency
That we choose.
To do the things
That God would have us do.
Or to use it,
To serve but only you.
If you but do
That which is right.
He will, with all his might.
Endow you with Power
To join the fight.
To prepare the way
For even Greater Light.

Who taught men to chain the lightning? Did man unaided
of himself discover that? No, he received the knowledge
from the Supreme Being. From him, too, has every art
and science proceeded, although the credit is given to this
individual, and that individual. But where did they get the
knowledge from, have they it in and of themselves? No.
Brigham Young

Embrace Your Divinity

All ye sons and daughters of God.
I urge ye,
To embrace your divinity.
The potential of which you hold,
Can lead you to lay hold
Upon the prizes of Eternity
And to the fullness of your destiny.
Study hard and be bold
In matters of righteousness
Of which you have been told.
As you do,
Your beauty will grow.
As you enlarge the matters
That you need to know.
Matters of great import,
To your Eternal soul.
Study all of that which Jesus told,
And the prophets of both new and old.
Listen and learn

And as you begin to understand
Your soul will begin to yearn
For more of God's love,
As you begin to feel
His Spirit burn.

God sent you here to prepare for a future greater
than anything you can imagine.
Dieter F Uchtdorf

———— ᴍᴏᴄᴏᴛᴏᴏᴍ ————

Great Reason

Oh what joy the journey holds
For he, whom to follow Jesus, chose.
Such treasure along the way,
Will he find everyday!
There are endless lessons to learn!
The answers he can know,
By asking God himself,
And turning unto him, every thought
And listening above all else.
To which he will receive, a stupor of thought,
If it be, a thing of naught.
But if it be right, then you surely will,
In his bosom, he will surely feel,
I mighty burning, from within,
Giving you cause, to thank Great and Mighty him.

Gratitude is the gateway to joy!
Elaine S Marshall

One Day

My God,
Your ways are Wise!
Your purposes are Glorious!
Because of you
My Heart is Joyous!
I wish to learn of all your ways!
So in your church here will I stay!
Please bless with time,
The time i will need,
To prepare my Heart and soul
To be ready to meet,
Up in Heaven
With you and Mother
But most of all
With my beloved Brother.

It is not how you start the race or where you are during the
race, it is how you cross the finish line that will matter.
Robert D Hales

The Wave Of Grace

If you wish to see Gods face,
You must ride the wave of Grace.
From Grace to Grace you must go,
Until all your flaws to you are known.
This is only the beginning,
There is still miles of road,
All uphill and winding,
To be travelled at Gods timing.
Conquer them all you must
If you wish to be,
Just as he commanded,
As perfect as me.

Grace is aid from on high to help us to become who God wants us to
be! It can come in the form of wisdom, knowledge, understanding,
strength and feelings through the Holy Ghost to enable us to grow.

Oh My Brethren

Oh my Brethren, my poor poor brethren.
Seek the spirit of God so you may find all the treasures.
Obey all the laws and seek him out,
To him tell all and your Heart pour.
Show him the love that he deserves,
And a place with him he will reserve.
He will tell you such wonderful things!

Knowledge that will make you cry while your Heart sings!
Search him so that in time you may,
Be prepared to live with him some day.

He will lift you up and place you on his
shoulders. He will carry you home.
Dieter F Uchtdorf

—⁓◦ₒ⁓◦⊙◦⁓ₒ◦⁓—

I Must Win This

I will only get out what I put in,
Whilst trying to free myself from sin.
With a Heart broken and a spirit contrite,
I am commanded to seek out the right.
Continuously in prayer crying out to him,
Working out my salvation with fear and trembling.
I am to turn all of my might,
My heart, my mind, my strength to him,
To conquer the evil one who tries constantly,
To sabotage my happiness and my divine destiny.
So I must pray to God unceasingly,
God teach me to conquer he whom I cannot see,
He whom desires me, an endless misery.

Pray always, that you may come off conqueror; yea, that
you may conquer Satan, and that you may escape the hands
of the servants of Satan that do uphold his work.
D&C 10:5

Perfection

Perfection is the objective of mortality!
How sad it is to see
That but a few pursue this opportunity.
To become as perfect like he who told us to be,
As perfect as the Father in Heaven and he!

Being the literal premortal children of the Father, you and I can,
by going from Grace to Grace, eventually receive the fulness of
the Father as Jesus did. In addition to being resurrected we can
become perfect, or in one set of meanings from the greek, finished,
completed and fully developed. But only if we worship (love) God
and Truly follow the example of our redeemer Jesus Christ. After
all Brothers and Sisters, the ultimate adoration is emulation.
Neil A Maxwell

Pray With The Heart

The prayer of the lips are heard by angels,
Who write them down and read them to God.
But the prayer of the Heart roars through Heaven
Like lightning and thunder.
It tears the fabric of space and time asunder,
It shakes Gods very throne,
And he feels what you feel,
All the way to his bones.
When your heart prays,
Know that it is not in vain,
For God hears and feels,
All of your pain.

Prayer is your personal key to Heaven!
Boyd K Packer

———— ∾⌇⌇⌇⌇⌇⌇⌇⌇⌇ ————

Joseph, Brigham and the Pioneers

To think that they only planted the seed,
The tree that will be I can hardly conceive.
Dreams and visions fill my heart,
Of the lamp that will light up the dark.
The stone cut out of the mountain without hands,
Destined to roll forth to consume all lands.
How Great oh God! How magnificent!
How spectacular it will be!

The Kingdom has come,
The Kingdom of the Mighty Son!
The Holy city soon to be!
While the rest of the world,
Evil will ravage.
Until they can finally take no more,
And to God's ways they will come to adore.

Thou sawest till that a stone was cut out without
hands, which smote the image upon his feet that were
of iron and clay, and brake them to pieces.
Daniel 2:34

—⁓⦿⁓—

My Master

My soul doth he stretch
As my heart strings he wrenches.
My spirit doth he nourish
And my mind he teaches.
Wisdom doth he feed me,
It is food for my Soul.
That I may learn to grow up
And not just grow old.

Repentance is a process of addition not subtraction.
Unknown

—⁓⦿⁓—

A Talent Please!

Dearest Daddy!
May I ask this of thee!
Won't you teach me how to multiply!
This thing called money!
I sought not for it much before!
As your Spiritual Gifts were worth so much more!
But soon I will need it to care for the one!
The one I desire to share with all this fun!
So won't you please send me a talent to start!
And teach me to multiply it into ten!
That we may be provided sufficient for our needs!
And able to serve thee in both word and deed!

God wishes to bless us both spiritually and temporally.

The American Constitution

What an opportunity!
God has placed before me!
To fight for the freedoms and liberties
Of people just like you and me!
Why should I not be able to carry?
The fire power needed to protect me?
And why should I not be able to marry?
As many women as will agree
To have me as their husband for all Eternity!

And who wish to accompany
Me home to The Father,
Where we can live happily!
Forever and ever!
To bear an endless posterity!
And live together forever!
As an Eternal family!

Next to being one in worshipping God, there is nothing in this
world upon which this church should be more united than in
upholding and defending the constitution of the United States.
David O Mckay

Unless we members of the church do all we can to
preserve the freedoms we have, within the bounds of
the law of God, we will be held accountable.
Joseph Smith

"There is no need to be involved in the fight for freedom,
all you need to do is live the gospel." Of course this is
a contradiction, because we cannot fully live the gospel
and not be involved in the fight for freedom.
Ezra Taft Benson.

—⟅⟆⟅⟆⟅⟆⟅⟆⟅⟆—

The Wise Enthusiast

I know the church is true!
But what to do next I haven't a clue?

Where do I find all that I am suppose to do?
The scriptures you say?
Sure! I will study them everyday!
Anything else?
Of course! The words of the prophets!
And that of the living one's above all else!
Take the Holy Ghost to be my guide?
Boy I can't wait! It's going to be a ride!

Oh you have no idea!

The Faithful

The fog keeps them bogged,
But still they try,
As a beautiful seed of hope motivates them,
That one day they will find,
A treasure that was well worth their time.
They nurture and nourish this seed of hope,
Hoping it will grow into a tree.
These people are so sweet,
They have beautiful minds,
The pureness of their Hearts,
Is what sets them apart.
One day they will be rewarded
When their faith grows into a perfect knowledge,
And they will finally be able to see
Reality!

And now as I said concerning faith--faith is not to have a
perfect knowledge of things; therefore if ye have faith ye
hope for things which are not seen, which are true.
Alma 32:31

Wherefore, having this perfect knowledge of God,
he could not be kept from within the veil; therefore
he saw Jesus; and he did minister unto him.
Ether 3:20

———— ഇവസ്ഥ ————

The Repentant

With a broken Heart and a contrite spirit,
He repents continuously while praying to God,
"Please teach me to hold firm to the rod."
As God imparts his Grace to him,
His weaknesses are changed to strengths from within!
You best give up hating on him,
Because Gods Mighty hand has he taken
And he is destined to win!

For if they humble themselves before me, and have faith in me,
then will I make weak things become strong unto them.
Ether 12:27

———— ഇവസ്ഥ ————

The Unrepentant

They will never grow up,
They will only grow old,
And the miracle of forgiveness they will never know.
It takes strength and humility to admit ones weaknesses,
It can often be humiliating and embarrassing,
But just push through and I promise you,
You will find it rewarding and liberating!
He will set your Soul free, new heights you will find!
As God expands, your Heart and mind!
You will grow in intelligence and skill!
As this my friends,
Is Gods desired will!
To teach us to become Great like him!
All he requires,
Is for us, to forsake sin,
The more you forsake,
The more you will be blessed!
With hidden treasures of knowledge and wisdom,
And even the mysteries to his Kingdom.

Repentance is not punishment. It is the hope-
filled path to a more glorious future.
Richard G Scott

The Sincere Seeker

In his Heart he really tries,
For his God he is willing to die.
But of the fullness he falls short,
Not sure entirely how to grasp the rod,
And he doesn't know that he can just ask God.
The succour of Jesus and the Power of his Grace,
He richly desires to have a taste,
But the fog keeps him bogged,
And the devils work overtime doing their job.

If any of you lack wisdom, let him ask of God.
James 1:5

Sky Scrapers

He that buildeth his house on the rock!
Shall build Sky Scrapers for Eternity!
Endless shall be upon him!
Kingdoms! Dominions! And Glory!
Unceasing will be his Posterity!
This my friends will be!
My happily ever after story!

O Lord God Almighty, hear us in these our petitions, and
answer us from heaven, thy holy habitation, where thou sittest

enthroned, with glory, honor, truth, justice, judgement, mercy,
and an infinity of fulness, from everlasting to everlasting.
D&C 109:77

The Hypocrites

They use to go to church but not any more,
Because of the flaws in everyone that they saw.
All they see are the motes in their brethren's eyes,
While asking not: "what is this beam that is in mine?"
They will hold you to the laws
That they themselves follow no more,
And laugh and point scorn at you
From that building next door.

If you define hypocrite as someone who fails to perfectly
live up to what he or she believes, we're all hypocrites.
Dieter F Uchtdorf

Residents Of The Great And Spacious Building

So great and spacious is the building,
With so many things to see and do,
Yet for a reason unknown to them,
They choose to stay and make fun of me and you.

The laughter of the world is merely loneliness trying to reassure itself.
Neal A Maxwell

"Like the throng of the ramparts of the "great and spacious building," they are intensely and busily preoccupied, pointing fingers of scorn at the steadfast iron-rodders. Considering their ceaseless preoccupation, one wonders, Is there no diversionary activity available to them, especially in such a large building – like a bowling alley? Perhaps in their mockings and beneath the stir are repressed doubts of their doubts."
Neal A. Maxwell

Isn't it odd that most people who are on the road to the Telestial Kingdom can often be seen laughing at the saints as they ride the front seat of the bus there. singing songs of mockery and sarcasm, laughing and pointing at the giant bill boards that read 'warning' 'danger ahead' and shouting at the driver to go faster. So sad isn't it.

The Lost

These poor souls, wondered have they,
For various reasons, in Zion, they no longer stay.
They have left the safety of the shelter,
To venture into the stormy bad weather.
Some are unaware of its bitter cold,
While others just love to play, in its dirty snow.
Trading the Celestial prize, for evils deceiving guise.
One can only hope they find their way home.

Stay in the boat!
The experienced river guides today can be likened
to the Church's apostles and prophets. They help
us arrive safely to our final destination.
M Russell Ballard

The Priesthood Are Asleep

Where are the Elijahs who rain fire from Heaven?
Where are the Moses that part the Mighty Sea?
Where are the Jesus's who make the blind see?
Where are the Moroni's who free those in captivity?
Where are the Alma's whose tongues are as sharp as a sword?
Where are the Brother of Jared's who have eyes to see?
Through the veil and into Eternity?
Where are the Nephi's who have power to shock?
Where are the Enoch's whom nobody dares to mock?

Where are the Isaiah's whose tongue is loosed with prophecy?
Where are the Solomons whose wisdom is exceeding?
Where are the Samson's who can overpower ten men?
Where are the Striplin Warriors who cause their enemies to tremble?
Where are the Snows who can travel between worlds?
Where are those worthy of transfiguration?
Where are they? Where are they? Where are they?
Father I pray that you give these to me,
That I may use these Gifts to be of service to thee.

If you will ask of me you shall receive.
D&C 6:5

———∿∿◦◦◦◦◦◦∿∿———

Oh Dear

Everywhere I look this is what I see!
People sucking each other with lies and sympathy,
Lips that do practice the arts of flattery and trickery.
I see little decision making being done;
"To my God! I wish to be one!"
And if there is and it is sad to see,
The decision only lasts until the footy.
"Hold on God! I will return! My team is playing! Wait your turn!"
"OK now, where were we? Oh yes that's right!
I wish to be one with thee!"
"Oh wait! Hang on again! My favourite show is on tv!"

And now, my beloved brethren, I desire that ye should remember

these things, and that ye should work out your salvation with fear
before God, and that ye should no more deny the coming of Christ.
Alma 34:37

————〜〜•〜〜————

This Is Love

Can you handle my words of truth?
Can you handle the Power of the Priesthood?
Have you ever seen words so crisp and clean?
I hear in your hearts you think me mean?
Would you rather I left you to slumber?
Until the morning when God your name calls?
Why did you not become one with me?
When you agreed to come and follow me?
You even covenanted that you would?
The promises were simple how could you have misunderstood?
You said you would listen to my Holy Prophets?
Obey my commandments and feel and see?
Why did you then not turn your every thought unto me?
That through my Spirit I might have lead and directed thee?
Did you think I was joking? Why did you take this lightly?
Now your probation is over, what ye think is a reward fitting for thee?

See the parable of the ten virgins.

It is impossible for a man to be saved in ignorance.
D&C 131:6

————〜〜•〜〜————

The Tourist

He comes, he goes,
Where he will end up,
Nobody knows.
His Heart may be crafted out of solid gold,
But his mind just wanders
Which ever way the wind blows.
With his holiday house in Babylon,
He sometimes comes home to Zion on weekends.

Let us once and for all establish our residence in Zion
and give up the summer cottage in Babylon.
Neal A Maxwell

Light Minded

They laugh and joke as they search for him,
As though they are not lost, and have no need of him.
The teachings of the gospel are taken lightly,
They enjoy eating, drinking, being loud and merry.
They realise not fully the terms of their probation,
Instead in their Hearts they think they are on vacation.

Therefore, cease from all your light speeches, from all
laughter, from all your lustful desires, from all your pride
and light-mindedness, and from all you wicked doings.
D&C 88:121

The Proud

Destined to be burnt as stubble,
It would be better for him to be humble.
More he doesn't need for Everything does he know,
And all of his sentences end with 'See! I told you so'.
Teach him you cannot, for he is no man's student.
In his own head, he is anything but prudent.
The path to Celestial Glory he is sure he has found,
And mistaken he could not be for he is too proud.
The whisperings of the spirit he listens to not,
Neither does he understand fully the teachings of the Iron Rod.

You have to learn from the Holy Ghost for only he can show you the
way! Don't know how? Its simple! Just ask God and he will show you!

The Modern Day Pirate

The web is his ocean,
He surfs it by night.
Scouring to find
Treasures and delights.
Against the law he puts up a fight,
As he struggles to download everything in his sight.
"I am no thief," you will here him cry,
But we will see when he meets Jesus after he dies.

This is probably the most common way citizens of Zion
loose their privileges. If you want revelation you must
be at least trying to keep the commandments.

The Serpent

Who needs enemies when you have friends like these,
Smile to your face and say things to please,
To your surprise their just lying in wait,
For the opportunity to deter you from entering the Gate.

A serpent is a sly or crafty person who seeks to win your trust with
the intention of betraying it or using it for ill without your knowing.

The Wolf In Sheep's Clothing

He will pretend to be your friend,
With the aim of leading you back to his den.
Flattery and security he offers you,
Till your right where he wants you.
Little by little he will lead you away,
Until from the flock you have strayed.
Once your trust is his you will begin to notice
The mistake that you made,
Now too little, too late.

Choose your friends with caution.
Thomas S Monson

The Social Butterfly

I go to church but I don't really know why,
It's something to do to past the time.
If there's an activity I will be there,
But mention scripture study and I don't really care.
The Gospel to me is a good story,
It gives me a good excuse to have a party.
Oh Jesus, yes! I know him!
Isn't he that guy, who died for our sins?
I must remember to say this,
If I wish to fit in!

We must come to church with a yearning for learning.

—∿∿◦◦❧◦❦◦∿∿—

The Silly

An endless chest of treasure they have found,
Sprawled open upon the ground.
Free for all who wish to partake,
As much as you want you can take.
But glancing casually upon it with their stares,
They desire not that it be all theirs.
Happy are they with one or two pieces,
They desire not the fullness of its riches.
Upon the gold do they stare,
Without so much as even a care.
'I have enough' in their Hearts do they say,
And they prepare themselves not for the Great and dreadful day.

Wo be unto him that shall say: We have received the word of God,
and we need no more of the word of God, for we have enough!
2 Nephi 28:29

—∿∿◦◦❧◦❦◦∿∿—

So Close Yet Not Quite

Doctrinally rich but developmentally poor.
So much work do they put in,
But yet they are still so far from him.
They study hard the things of God,
But still are not grasping the Iron Rod.
The application of the scriptures,
They cannot do,
Because they refuse to ask you know who.

You have to be shown how to keep the commandments from the
Holy Ghost, this privilege you will receive as you ask the Father
for this and try. There are so many! How do you think you can be
successful at keeping them all - and at the same time - relying on
your own strength and wisdom? Ask him to teach you right now!

Trust in the Lord with all your Heart and lean
not unto thine own understanding.
Proverbs 3:5

———∿∾⊙⋇⊙∾∿———

The Contentious

The last word they must always have,
Every argument must be won.
Forgiveness? Letting go?
What's that?
Instead,

I will crush you like a train!
Leave you in a world of pain!
To me this is one big game,
And if you want to play,
Beware, I am untamed.

He that hath the spirit of contention is not of me, but is of the
devil, who is the father of contention, and he stirrers up the
Hearts of men to contend with anger, one with another.
3 Nephi 11:29

———⁓〰⦿〰⦿〰——

The Buffetiers

Oh this looks good I will do that!
No this doesn't sit forget about that!
They pick and choose like they are at a buffet,
Taking only those doctrines that to them are gourmet.
They think themselves to be God
What did you say?
I will tell you what is good Lord.
As if the Universe is theirs,
And to Gods Throne they are guaranteed heirs.
An ignorance it seems stems from within,
As they pick and choose doctrine thinking that will get them in.
If you want to go where God lives,
Do you not think that you should listen to him?
To his servants the Prophets and Apostles?
The ones that he personally called and chose?

Whatever God requires is right, no matter what it is, although we
may not see the reason thereof until long after the events transpire.
Joseph Smith

———— ·•∞∞⟨◦⟩∞∞•· ————

The Confused

They see good as evil and evil as good,
Totally confused, they understand not the Rod.
They go after their own imaginations and learn not from the Spirit,
When asked how they came to that conclusion,
They proudly answer with "I did it!"
We are here to discern between truth and error,
By taking every thought unto he,
As you feel and see.
Allow him to teach you, why do it on your own?
Stop thinking in your head that you already have your own Throne.
How can you expect to become like him,
If you don't humble yourself and ask of him?
Ask him to teach you to understand,
Of the scriptures and of his Great plan!

Look unto me in every thought
D&C 6:36

———— ·•∞∞⟨◦⟩∞∞•· ————

The Incredulous

The truth is so large! So different from this world!
It can be hard to comprehend! It can make your mind swirl!
Sometimes no matter how much you want to you still cannot grasp!
The nature of God and all that he has!
So what do you do if through the veil you cannot see?
For it can only mean that you are still not knowing.
For if you had a perfect knowledge then you would see,
Just how big! Is Eternity!
Water the seed that you have planted!
Nourish it all day! By letting the Spirit lead and guide the way!
Ask him in the mornings:
"My God! What are we doing today!?"

Wherefore, having this perfect knowledge of God,
he could not be kept from within the veil; therefore
he saw Jesus; and he did minister unto him.
Ether 3:20

The Early Finisher

I believe! I believe!
There is nothing more, for me to see!
My dear friend have you even,
Caught a glimpse, of the Celestial Kingdom?
Have you seen through the veil?
And been allowed to tell the tale?

Have you had your calling and election made sure?
Where Jesus visits you, and gives you three cheers?
If you answered no to the above,
Then there is still more that you should do.
Start by getting to know him,
Until you come to love him,
And don't forget, to purify yourself before him.

Wherefore, having this perfect knowledge of God,
he could not be kept from within the veil; there fore
he saw Jesus; and he did minister unto him
Ether 3:20

The Half Hearted

The spirit they have but they talk to it not,
It seems the greatest gift to man they just simply forgot.
They see the world through their own point of view,
And seek not for council from you know who.
If you want to be a God then from whom should you learn?
You should take him every thought then feel the spirit burn!
Unto what end you ask?
Until you are purified before him at last!

Turn unto me your every thought
D&C 6:36

The Heart Of The Natural Man

His Heart has many seasons,
The cause being total confusion,
For he controleth not his soul,
And he is not his own.
Instead he is acted upon,
By Devils who cheer him on.
Leading him astray,
Into states of disarray.

He that is slow to anger is better than the mighty; and
he that ruleth his spirit than he that taketh a city.
Proverbs 16:32

The Idler

Always doing something, but never really doing anything,
His priorities are in desperate need of reordering.
Not having a clue, or just not wanting to do,
He hibernates himself in the madness of time.
Progression to them is a stranger,
And they do not realise that they are in danger.
Like the unprofitable servant who buried his talent,
Of suffering reprimand or worse, damnation.
Study the scriptures and ponder a lot,
And pray to God to teach you the Rod.

It is possible to be busy all the time, yet busy doing
nothing of an Eternal nature. Real progression comes from
receiving revelation from Mr Holy Ghost on that which
you need to improve, here a little and there a little.

Living Beneath Your Privileges

This is perhaps the most common in Zion,
People don't understand what is going on,
Because that which matters most they cannot see,
I am talking about the Holy Ghost and the things of Eternity.
They know that he is real but understand not,
The significance of this really great gift,
And how he can prepare you to one day meet God!
And teach to you, more then alot!
If you would but turn unto him,
Your every thought.

Turn unto me your every thought.
D&C 6:36

Living Beneath Your Privileges 2

They don't pray for Grace,
Oh what a waste.
Nor do they do,
All that they can do.
Why do they choose
To misuse their agency,
And miss out on this wonderful opportunity?
To sore to heights unimaginable!
That to the mortal mind,
Are unfathomable!

Grace is help from on high to make you better!
Like Nephi acknowledged when he wrote,
which of you by taking thought can add one cubit unto his stature?
3 Nephi 13:27

Living Beneath Your Privileges 3

They search not the scriptures,
Nor bother to learn all the rules.
Instead on their own wisdom do they rely,
And nobody but themselves do they fool.
I pray they'll awake and realise the need,
And to all the warnings they take heed,
Because it clearly says that you need to learn,
Or of that Great reward you will not earn.

It is impossible for a man to be saved in ignorance.
D&C 131:6

Living Beneath Your Privileges 4

They neither knock, nor ask,
They rely on their own understanding.
They turn to him only some of their Heart,
might, mind and strength.
They turn unto him only some of their thoughts.
They do not feel and see the things of the world,
Nor of themselves.
They seek not to be of one Heart, mind and purpose
with the Holy Ghost - the mind of God.
They are only partially penitent.
Thus living beneath their privileges, wasting their
probation and not fulfilling their potential.
Therefore they are not of the few there be that find it.

Because strait is the gate, and narrow is the way, which
leaders unto life, and few there be that find it.
Mathew 7:14
And if you want to find it, who do you think you should ask to lead
you to it? Lead me, guide me, walk beside me, help me find the way!

Lovers Of The Word But Deniers Of The Spirit

They can recite entire passages,
And have every handbook memorised.
But seek not their understanding from God,
Nor ask him to teach them how to hold properly onto the Iron Rod.
Instead, after their own interpretations do they rely,
And in their Hearts, to God they are shy.

The only way to become successful at keeping all the commandments
is to ask the Father to have the Holy Ghost teach you how! Line upon
line and precept upon precept, here a little and there a little! And
as you journey through your day, you will begin to **feel** him say.

The Defensive

Often they cry,
"What about you! What about you!"
As if somehow it changes the truth.
Embarrassed, they seek to shift the blame,
Not taking responsibility they continue playing games.
Never admitting thus never repenting,
Unless they change,
These poor souls are destined to stay the same.

The first step of repentance is to admit. Then the rest can follow, be sorry, change, and don't do it again! ABCD

The Defensive 2

The truth is often hard to hear,
For it pierces the soul like a spear.
But instead of taking responsibility and repenting,
They get angry and start cussing.
Repentance is fun! Exciting! And rewarding!
It takes you to places you cannot even imagine!
So admit your flaws and ask God to tell you all!
Then allow his enabling power,
To improve you every hour!

Repentance is simply the process of becoming better! Is not a purpose of the Gospel to make a bad man good and a good man better? Wouldn't you like to be better?

The Proud

They care more about being right than what is right.
When they are wrong the truth for these is hard to bear.
They would rather continue living lives of despair,

Than to enter into the path of repentance,
The road to Eternal Life and Exaltation.
Unless they humble themselves they will not find,
The treasure that awaits at the end of time.

There are many types of behaviour that can slow or even completely
dam your progression, with this in mind you should just ask God!
And once he helps you to overcome them, your progression can
be speedy! And you can begin to make some real progress!

Living In Denial

They know the truth when they hear it,
But still they argue against it.
Pride won't let them change,
Despite knowing the errors of their ways,
Darkness surrounds them,
As they pretend to be unfazed.
Unless they pray, they will remain the same.

Which of you by taking thought can add one cubit unto his stature?
3 Nephi 13:27

The Self Righteous

These people like to feel that they are better than you,
By highlighting all the wrong things that you do.
While little attention do they give,
To what's in their own eye and the size of it.
Often our own flaws are hard to see,
So cry out to God to show you all.
And he will reveal them to you slowly,
Otherwise you would be overwhelmed completely.

It is a common thing for us to be completely ignorant of all of our
own flaws, ask God to show you and you will see what I mean!
He will show them to you slowly and after quite some time you
will be like: "Oh my Goodness God! Please! Make me Holy!"

—⁓∿◦◦⌒◦⌒◦◦∿⁓—

The Self-righteous 2

Yet again this is so common,
The sufferers of mote-beam sickness.
They pick on you while not having a clue,
Of their own faults they are not only unaware,
But more than often, they don't even care!
They make up the rules as they go along,
The example being not Christ but they themselves.

You don't make progression by focusing on others, my advise
to you? See if that behaviour that you can see in others is

apparent in yourself! For more than often that which annoys
us the most is common in ourself! Ask God! He will show
you! Then don't forget to ask him to improve you!

———— ⟊⟊⟊⟊⟊⟊⟊ ————

The Human Condition

Look at that man! He's so smart!
But oh wait! Compared to God, no he's not!
We are all like little children with little understanding,
Who need to be taught, the ways of the Rod.
Nobody ever grasps it entirely on their first go,
And nobody will do so properly without help from the Holy Ghost.
So don't be embarrassed everyone is struggling,
But keep in mind, nobody will reach perfection
unless they are really trying.
Never think you know it all because that's when you'll fail to see,
All the important things that are yet to be!
So grow from Grace to Grace until your completed,
Perfected, finished, and your sins depleted.
Thus the fullness of the Father you will have received!
Finally becoming as Great as he wants you to be!
Yea, even as he!

There is no other one item that will so much astound
you, when your eyes are opened in Eternity, as to
think that. You were so stupid in the body.
Brigham Young

———— ⟊⟊⟊⟊⟊⟊⟊ ————

The Blank Minded

They are not very articulate,
So they get easily frustrated,
Not able to own how they feel,
They quickly become angry and ill.
Quick to throw tantrums,
They make sure you know how they feel,
My dear friend, God is your magic pill!!!
What he is doing for me, he can do for you!
Once upon a time, I was angry like you!
Until I turned unto him my every thought,
And prayed to him, more than alot.
He teaches me so slowly, through the Holy Ghost,
And is growing my intelligence more than most!
Line upon line, precept upon precept,
He teaches me, infinity!!!
So pray to him and take his hand!
And if you happen to pass me,
Then hooray my friend!!!
But don't get angry and not heed this advice,
For you'll get left behind if you have to think twice!!

Every displeasurable feeling can be permanently overcome with
understanding. Where do I get this understanding you might ask!
Why! From Mr Holy Ghost why of course! Where else! Little by little,
here a little, there a little, just ask Heavenly Father for this privilege!

He that is void of wisdom despiseth his neighbour:
but a man of understanding holdeth his peace.
Proverbs 11:12

The Unconscious

Unaware of their unconscious state,
I pray they'll awake before it grows to late.
Their eyes are open but they cannot see,
Many of the things of Eternity.
Stuck are they in heart and mind,
Consumed by the mighty wrath of time.
They have ears but cannot hear,
All that which the Gods treasure dear,
To truth, knowledge and wisdom they are a stranger,
Unaware of the impending danger.
Unless the Gospel they do accept,
And to the laws they keep in check,
Take the Spirit to be their guide,
They will miss out on this awesome ride.

There is a difference between hearing and listening, reading and
understanding. Mr Holy Ghost can teach you understanding!
Ask the Father for this privilege and don't forget you asked!

Hear now this O foolish people who are without understanding,
which have eyes, and see not, which have ears, and hear not.
Jeremiah 5:21

The Wise Man Of Zion

You'll never learn wisdom relying on your own understandings,
We are all learning from one spirit or the other,
Either growing close to God or further.
Social correctness can often be unwise,
For you are often trying to please devils in disguise.
What is right and what is wrong is defined by God,
All the way down to the smallest of thoughts.
You may not understand fully what I mean
But hearken to the spirit and you will,
For my dear friends, turning every thought unto him,
Is like taking the red pill.

Trust in the Lord with all thine heart; and lean
not unto thine own understanding.
In all thy ways acknowledge him, and he shall direct thy paths.
Proverbs 3:5-6

The Assumers

To lazy to study the scriptures properly,
They rely on their own understanding.
When faced with a problem they think in their hearts,
If I were God what would I do?
Hey that sounds right to me! It must be true!
To the Spirit they are shy,
Come Judgement day they will cry.

Unless they pray:
"God make me wise!"

To become successful at properly understanding the scriptures,
Mr Holy Ghost must teach them to you, here a little and
there a little. Ask Heavenly Father for this privilege.

It is impossible for a man to be saved in ignorance.
D&C 131:6

Trust in the Lord with all thine heart; and lean
not unto thine own understanding.
Proverbs 3:5

———— ~~~~~~~~~~ ————

The Ignorantly Confident

They seem so sure and without the Spirit can be hard to see,
The depth of ignorance that lies within he.
Especially when he laughs and smiles,
And easily manages to convince you that all is well.
"Don't worry boy! You will see!"
"All is well! There is no need to worry!
"Just partake of the ordinances!"
"There is no need to be one with he!"
"When we die we will all inherit a Celestial Glory!"
Do not believe this Devils flattery,
His lies will cost you your Celestial Glory.

If everyone goes to the Celestial Kingdom, then why is there
a Terrestrial Kingdom? The Celestial is for those who really
tried their hardest, the Terrestrial is for those who didn't.

Therefore wo be unto him that is at ease in Zion!
Wo be unto him that crieth: All is well!
2 Nephi 28:24-25

The Stupidly Confident

Take a scripture they will,
And ask not the Holy Ghost to interpret.
Instead Devils they will listen to,
Learning it's meaning incorrect.
Usually also laziness and short term memory they befriend,
Having not read or forgotten what the other scriptures meant.
They cling to the ones that by twisting will support their view,
While conveniently forgetting the ones that will take work to do,
And then try to use them to influence you!
Beware the stupidly and ignorantly confident,
Their masses have grown!
There are most likely armies of them near your home!
Do not be deceived by their flattery and ease!
These stupid confident appearing people have been deceived!
I do not ask you to trust me either,
Instead I say! To go to your knees and pray pray pray!
That Heavenly Father through his Spirit!
Will this day show to you the way!
But don't forget this!

Prayer without further study,
Tends to avail nobody.
Good day!

And because he speaketh flattering words unto you, and he
saith that all is well, then ye will not find fault with him.
Helaman 13:28

The Two Minute Pastors

The praise of man they desire more than wisdom.
You can tell them and tell them but they just won't listen.
Come to my church and pay me your offerings,
And in return I will shower you with assurance!
You are saved, your debt Jesus paid!
The irony is they do not lie, yet are leading you astray.
Led into a false sense of security you think you
are ok, for the pastor has told you,
God loves you, it's ok.
His words are true though he doth not lie,
God does love you, but he wants you to try!
To become like him! To overcome all!
So that you may live in the Heaven the highest of all!

Why do I call them two minute pastors? Because they can teach
everything they know about God in under two minutes. They receive
no new revelations. Some teach for the love of God, others for riches
and glory, others just know not the truth. Though most may have
good intentions, they are teaching incomplete or incorrect doctrine.

I knew a man in Christ above fourteen years ago, (whether in
the body, I cannot tell; or whether out of the body, I cannot tell:
God knoweth;) such an one caught up to the third Heaven.
2 Corinthians 12:2

He that overcometh shall inherit all things; and I
will be his God, and he shall be my son.
Revelations 21:7

—⁓◦⌒⟨⟩◦⌒⟨⟩⟨⟩⟨⟩◦⌒⟨⟩◦⁓—

The Flattering Devil

Of one heart and one mind with the stupid and ignorantly confident,
The flattering idiot with his sweet talk and velvet lips likes to lie.
Unknowing to you he is a viscous and cunning predator,
His meal is your heart and winning your trust is his game,
There is no real good reason for this,
Only to add to his fortune and fame.
He starts by telling you that all is well,
But fear not for I am no devil, I will tell you that there is a hell!
He would never however tell you the things you need to repent,
Because firstly he lives in so much darkness he is too blind to see,
And secondly that would give you a reason to be mad at he.
And that would not bring him fame, fortune and glory,
Thus defeating his purposes, so he continues to lie to thee.
And you will believe him because of his confidence and charm,
And the soft, gentle words that he uses to disarm.
Though he may not realise it,
He is raining upon you danger and harm.

And others will he pacify, and lull them away into carnal
security, that they will say: All is well in Zion; yea, Zion
prospereth, all is well. And thus the devil cheateth their
souls, and leadeth them away carefully down to hell.
And behold, others he flattereth away, and telleth them there
is no hell; and he saith unto them: I am no devil, for there is
none--and thus he whispereth in their ears, until he grasps them
with his awful chains, from whence there is no deliverance.
2 Nephi 28:21-22

The Fool

Leave the fool alone in his folly,
Ignore him, and don't join him,
Least you end up in his trolley.
Though he may come across as rather jolley,
Join him not but leave him in his folly.
Try and correct him but don't try to hard,
For a fool is a fool and correcting him is hard.
Attention is what he craves
And the more you give him
The more that way he will stay.

The folly of fools is deceit.
Proverbs 14:8

The Aggressive Sloth

O so common and so sad to see,
These poor people are just so lazy.
And as if that weren't enough,
They will go far out of their way,
To twist the truth so that where they are they can stay.
Any excuse they will use to get out of a re-study,
And satans greatest trick they like to play,
Twisting the scriptures to suit their easy ways.
"Look at this one it means this!"
"Forget about that one! There's no need for it!"
"I have enough! I know it all!"
"What does that boy know!"
"Do you know how long I have been a member for!"
They don't bother consulting the Spirit, they don't even ask,
It is too much trouble, they would rather just sit, point and laugh.

You must take the Holy Ghost to be your teacher! It is so
important and rewarding! The more attention you try to
give him the more attention he will give you in return!

———∿∿◦◦◦∿∿———

Redemption!

It is so liberating
To express myself!
I really like the concept of honesty!

To say how I feel and to feel what I say!
Shouldn't speak it?
Well I shouldn't be thinking it!
God can read your mind and even your Heart!
If your having naughty thoughts then you better start,
Seeking his help on this is what you are here for.
For by your thoughts you will be judged in his court.
You can try to hide, but to no avail,
For do you think God will believe airy tales?

For our words will condemn us, yea, all our works
will condemn us; we shall not be found spotless;
and our thoughts will also condemn us.
Alma 12:14

Short Stories

A Gift of Grace

The lowly garbage collector rolled along,
Picking up the trash while signing his song.
In the shadow he saw something shining,
He shouted with a Heart full of joy,
Oh boy! What timing!
On the shiny box the label read Grace,
The lowly garbage man had a puzzled look on his face.
He opened the box and saw that it was empty,
Except for a note that on it wrote;
I am God the Father of your Spirit,
I give you this gift I hope you will receive it.
It is a Power that I give to you,
To help you become anything that you want to.
All you have to do is ask of me,
Obey my commandments and I will strengthen thee.
Anything that you ask I will grant to you,
So long as I see that it is good for you.
Excited and enthused the lowly garbage man cried:
"Help me God to be more than I."
I drive around everyday day in this smelly truck,
And they only pay me ten lousy bucks.
I have a family of ten to feed,
Do you know how much these kids eat!

I hear your cries my faithful son,
Open your eyes and look around,
I will open a door for you.
To do that which you desire to do.

A few years went by till we met again,
When I saw him he started to cry.
He wept and he cried with tears in his eyes,

The lowly garbage collector now in a suit and tie.
He told me the story of what God did for him,
He said all he did was knock and God took him in.
He taught me through the still small voice,
I really had to listen over all of the noise.
He helped me to study and even improved my memory!
I could learn anything and remember everything!
Thanks to the gift of Grace that God gave me!
I am so happy because now I can feed my family!
My kids all have new shoes and clothes to wear!
And tomorrow we are all going to the fair!
Thanks to the gift of Grace that God gave me!
I can now take care of my family!

A Little Story

From dust to Glory,
This is a story.
Of a boy who was immersed,
In the ways of this Earth.
Miserable was he,
And endless it was.
For Gods laws, he understood, not at all.
Neither did he, have the Spirit of He,
To guide and aid him along on his journey.
Into every dead end, did this man travel.
Scratching his head, trying to find,
A corner of the world, where happiness existed,
Little did he know, that he was just being tested.

Then one day the gates opened,
Not the pearly ones though that he was hoping.
Devils rushed him and tried to deceive,
Told him they were friends, and to come follow me.
But this man was so distrusting,
Not even the Devil's charm did he believe.
The Devil got mad and tried harder and harder,
Flattering him with lies, so that his trust he might win.
Not long passed until God finally stepped in,
And showed to him the love that he had unknowingly yearned.
The man collapsed and cried aloud,
Oh Great God, what must I do,
So that more of your Love, I can earn?

This is my church my son,
Come and learn, to with me be one.
Study hard and learn all that I have revealed,
So that one day, to me, you will be sealed.
I have prepared a place for you,
But first to me, you must prove yourself true.
I know you can do it, I know you will.
So just be patient. I'll make you this deal.
Come work for me and do my will,
Do all that I bid and I make this promise to you.
All that you desire, I will make come true.
I will seal you with fire, to all whom you admire.
All of this, because I love you.

Earth has no sorrow that Heaven cannot cure.
Dallin H Oaks

A Made up Story

"Want to hear a made up story!!"

"Sure!"

"Ok then!"

I once asked a Christian Pastor to tell me everything
he knew about God and how to get to Heaven!! It took
two minutes. and he kept repeating himself.
Kept yelling at me: "Grace! Grace! We are saved by Grace!"

Then!!!

I heard the templars knew the mysteries of Earth and their bosses
even knew how to get to Heaven!! ... using technology!! ...

Then I realised that this is cheating.

And they only knew how to get to one of the lowest Heavens anyway

(Sigh) All that excitement I thought they really had something

Verily, verily, I say unto you, He that entereth not by the door
(ordinances and refinement through the Power of the Holy
Ghost until you receive the fullness) into the sheepfold, but
climbeth up some other way, the same is a thief and a robber.
But he that entereth in by the door is the shepherd of the sheep.
And are going to get kicked out come the time.
(John 10:1-2)

So I asked the Illuminati if they knew what to do to get to Heaven!

They confidently shouted back:

"NOTHING!! This is a computer game!! Which team do you want to join!! I'm going to be Darth Vadar in the next world! Who do you want to be? We are here to experience! Anything and Everything! Just Go Wild and Pig out on your every desire!"

"Oh! Enticing!" I thought

"How do you know that may I ask?"

"A little grey guy told me! Would you like to meet him? He knows everything!"

"Do you trust him?"

"Yes! He has a really cool spaceship and he says that he is my frrrriiiieeeennnnd! And that is good enough for me!!"

So I went to the Catholic Church and asked them.

"I will Sprinkle some water on your forehead! Confess your sins every week say three Hail Mary's and you will be fine"

I thought to myself, "ok that is not a lot."

So I thought I would shop around a little longer.

"Mr Muslim Sir! What do I need to do to go to Heaven!"

"You need to live an honourable life!"

"Hmm very nice! But still so simple."

Then I saw a Buddhist monk walking and
asked him how do I get to Heaven!

He told me there was no Heaven, and, and, I have to come back here.

I remembered the time I was told there was no Santa.

So after I dried my eyes, I met a Mormon!

"Mormon! What do I need to do to go to Heaven"

"Do you have an hour?"

"An hour?" I asked.

"Yes"

First he told me how 'Mormon' was just a nick name after the
book of Mormon and that this is The Church of Jesus Christ!
Restored! Then he told me how after Jesus and his Apostles
were killed there was no more church on the Earth hence all
the different churches and a need for a restoration and also
about the story of Joseph Smiths similar predicament of not
knowing which Church to join. and then he said to me:

"Now let us kneel down and ask of God that he might
make known to you if what I say is true."

"Ask God!"

"Why what a good idea! Why did I not
think to do that in the first place"
- I spoke within so as not to come across as a fool

So I asked.

"Father in Heaven" (as He instructed) "Is what this man says
true" "In the name of Jesus Christ Amen" (Again as he instructed)

Feelings of comfort and joy filled my Being and I begun to cry

"Does this mean I'm going to Heaven???"

"This means that Heavenly Father has prepared a way
for you to return to live with him again. But there is
much to learn. it will take quite some time."

So five years of non stop learning passed and still the same reply.

"There is much to learn. it will take time."

And when ye shall receive these things, I would exhort you that
ye would ask God, the Eternal Father, in the name of Christ, if
these things are not true; and if ye shall ask with a sincere heart,
with real intent, having faith in Christ, he will manifest the
truth of it unto you, by the power of the Holy Ghost. And by the
power of the Holy Ghost ye may know the truth of all things.

(Moroni 10:4-5)

"According to his perfect timing so remember that you asked"

"Thank you Mr Mormon. Thank you"

———∿᧒᧒᧒◇᧒᧒∿———

A story That Began In Heaven

Chapter 1

Childhood

"Mother! Mother! Father says we can go to earth soon! I'm going
to be just like him one day Mother! Just like him! You'll see!"
I could not keep the excitement contained within me! I was
ecstatic! The Father had just announced the news everybody
had been living to hear. The creation of the worlds had finally
begun! All of us spirit children would finally have the opportunity
to receive a body and a chance to prove ourselves worthy of
Godhood! Wow! The next stage of our eternal progression
was near! Everybody here has been looking forward to this for
ever! And the creations are now under way! How exciting!

This is the biggest news of my life! The chance to go to an
earth just as our parents had, to learn and to grow just as they
did, to become even as they! How cold shivers of awe and
excitement pierce my very spirit at the very thought of entering

into mortality. What wonders? What opportunities? What
lessons? What trials? What experiences await me? What great
and wonderful plan has The Father for me? What ever they
are, I expect them to be of a wise and most glorious nature!

I cannot think of anything else since The Fathers announcement
yesterday. Fantasies of my mortal experience have been occupying my
thoughts. I have been pondering the first stages of mortality. I will
be born into my brand new body created of the physical elements
just as our parents have! Oh boy! The first thing I will have to do
is to learn how to use it! Mother often recalls the excitement of
using her hands for the first time. She always talks about the joy
she felt from holding onto things such as fingers of other mortals.
Then there would be learning how to walk. Mother said she was
always falling over! She tells stories of when she first begun to crawl.
She says the memory loss of her existence prior to mortality made
everything all the more intriguing! "It's like everything was foreign
and new to me! I could never remember anything before my mortal
birth! I didn't even know that I existed before the world! The
world was so big and mysterious! Every where I went, everything
was new! It was an indescribable adventure! Just wait son! You will
see!" Mother always tells me stories of when she was in mortality in
one of the many worlds created under the decree of The Father.

Stage two of mortality after mastering the basic motor skills needed
is a bit of a mystery to me. I am not sure which dispensation or
on which planet I am to be born into. There will be many! News
of our entrance into mortality is still in the early days yet, I'd
dare say that The Father is still in the early stages of preparing
our individual plans. He and the other Gods have a great work
cut out for them. There are so many of us spirit children up here.
Yet he some how manages to know us all individually. It never
fails to amaze me that whenever he visits, he seems to know
everything that I have been doing! He often congratulates me
on my achievements before I even get the chance to tell him!

I have heard however, that usually and most probably I will
be able to experience being raised by parents all over again.
I also heard that there are some who will not. These receive
trials and tribulations of an entirely different nature - Heavenly
Father knows each of us personally and knows what we are in
need of learning. A bit of a concern amongst us spirit children
is that our parents are going to be each other! This causes me
to worry much, however I am often assured by mother that
the inadequacies of those having the role of parents will be
greatly beneficial to our mortal education and vice versa.

We are taught in mortality prep that there are endless combinations
of trials to face. All of vastly different natures and of different degrees
of intensities. When we were told this in class some of the students
started to tremble a little bit but when our teacher saw this, she very
lovingly assured us that The Father would not give us more than
we will be able to bear. And that if we are obedient and learn his
teachings - which will be made available to most of us - and seek
to follow the guidance and direction of the Holy Ghost, we will be
able to surmount anything that we face! Until we have conquered
all things and overcome the world in which we are placed, thus
becoming like 'The Father'. "The 'key' to success in mortality,"
she often repeats, "will be to develop a strong relationship with the
Holy Ghost and to study diligently the words of the prophets, they
will tell you all that you need to know and do. REMEMBER!"
She constantly stresses. "You will only get out what you put in, so
be sure to avoid the needless cares of the world your in, stay clear
of temptation, and be sure not to waste your time with distractions
that will have no significant benefit to your eternal progression.
There will be many, children. There will be many. So be watchful."

To be continued...

For the little Children

———∾∾◦◦◦∾∾———

I will be writing a lot more of these and they will
be used to teach the little children in Zion!

We Must Keep The Kitchen Clean!

I like to help to make the kitchen clean!
I like to help to do the dishes!
After dinner when we finish eating!
Me and my family have a big meeting!
We gather in the kitchen for a really big mission!
To clean up the mess that has been left!
Mummy and daddy cooks!
So I will help clean!
If i don't, it would be really mean!
I want to help to make the kitchen clean!

You Need To Love Me!

You need to love me mummy!
You need to love me daddy!
I am only very little!
So I need to know you love me!
I want you to hug me!
I want you to kiss me!
I want you to tell me!
Every day that you love me!
I need to know when I do wrong!
So that I can change and grow up strong!
But what I need the most!
Is for my mummy and daddy!

To tell me that they love me!
Everyday! Everyday! Everyday!

Let Us Do What Is Right

I will stand for what is right!
I will live to choose the right!
I will do so with all my might!
To the iron rod I will forever hold tight!
I will say my prayers every night!
Before I go to bed to Heavenly Father I will say goodnight!
And when I wake up I will again choose the right!

It Is Good To Be Kind

I like to be kind!
I like to be kind to people!
And animals too!
I like to give them hugs!
And kisses too!
I like to feed the animals at the zoo!
Because doing kind things make me feel good!
I try to be kind all the time!
Being kind includes sharing what is mine!

So if I have more than I need!
I like to share it with someone in need!

I Don't Like To Fight!

I don't like to fight!
Fighting isn't right!
Someone could get hurt if there is a fight!
If I see a fight I should try and stop it!
Somebody could get hurt if the fight doesn't stop!
I must tell an adult what is going on!
Even if the bad man is really strong!
I must do all that I can to stop the fight!
Somebody could get hurt!
Fighting is not right!

I Want To Be A Good Boy!

I want to be a good boy!
Because it is good to be good!
When I do good things I feel really good!
It makes me really happy to know that I am good!

So I want to be a good boy!
Because it is good to be good!

I Want To Be A Good Girl!

I want to be a good girl!
Because it is good to be good!
When I do good things I feel really good!
It makes me really happy to know that I am good!
So I want to be a good girl!
Because it is good to be good!

I Want To Be Like Jesus Mummy!

I want to be like Jesus mummy!
He has chariots of Fire!
And the most beautiful temples!
Angels serve him!
Devils fear him!
The streets are covered in gold where he lives!
And to everybody his love does he give!

I want to be like Jesus mummy!
I want to be like Jesus!

Mummy! Daddy!

Please tell me that you love me!
Please tell me that you care!
Mummy? Daddy?
Are you there?
I need to know you love me!
I need to know you care!
Please tell me that you love me!
Please tell me that you care!
I makes me feel so good inside!
To know that I am good!
Please tell me that you love me!
Please tell me that you care!
I must not take what is not mine!
I must not take what is not mine!
I must not steal!
Stealing is bad!
If I steal! People will get mad!
I will get in trouble with Mr Police Man!
He will take me away!
And I will have to live with all the bad men!
I must not steal!
Stealing is bad!

I Must Brush My Teeth After Every Meal!

I must brush my teeth after every meal!
If I don't brush my teeth they will get dirty!
Germs will grow there in my mouth!
They will live there in a dirty house!
All of this will be in my mouth!
When I speak my mouth will smell!
All because of the germs living in my mouth!
If I don't brush my teeth they will look yucky!
They will change colour and get really dirty!
They could rot away and could fall out!
All because of the germs that will live in my mouth!
So I must brush my teeth after every meal!
So the germs won't want to live in my mouth!

Oh Great God! Please Tell Me Your Plan!

Oh Great God! Please tell me your plan!
So me, mummy and daddy can understand!
Hi little one I am glad you want to know!
Let me tell you about a story from long ago!
Once upon a time on the planet you stay!
I sent you Jesus to show you the way!
Prophets he raised to teach the people Gods ways!

But many did not listen so they went the wrong way!
One day Jesus came down from Heaven!
To teach the people and to start Gods church!
But the people got angry and did not listen!
They were bad and they got really mad!
He tried to show a better way to live!
Through the commandments that God lovingly gave!
The people killed him and Gods church was destroyed!
Until not long ago when God called a little boy!
He was fourteen years old when he knelt before God!
And asked with his heart, "what should I do?"
God and his Son appeared to him!
And told him to start the church that your in!
Study hard little one and learn of my ways!
Listen to your teachers they will teach you the way!
So that you and your family can live with me one day!

Thank You God For Jelly And Jam!

I love to eat Jelly! I Love to eat Jam!
Sometimes for lunch, mummy makes me ham!
But what I really love is Jelly and Jam!
I like how they wiggle! It really makes me giggle!
Oh thank you God for Jelly and Jam!

Thank You God For This Brand New Day!

Thank you God for this brand new day!
For giving me more time to learn your ways!
Thank you dear God for teaching me to pray!
So that I can talk to you everyday!
Thank you dear God for showing me the way!
Through my teachers when I see them on Sunday!
Thank you God for a brand new day!
And for giving me more time with my friends to play!

Heavenly Father?

Heavenly Father can you come and visit with me?
Before I go to bed tonight,
Mummy and daddy will tuck me in tight!
They will read me a story like they do every night!
They will tell me that they love me and don't let the bed bugs bite!
Then they will close the door and be out of my sight!
I know my Heavenly Father will be by my side!
He comes to give me kisses in the night!
And tells me he loves me and hugs me tight!
I can never see him but I know he is there.
Because I can feel his spirit telling me he cares!

Thank You Mummy!

Thank you mummy for Mash and Peas!
Thank you mummy for cooking for me!
I really like all that you do for me!
But what I like most is your mash and peas!
Oh how I love them topped with gravy!
Thank you mummy for cooking for me!

I Love To Keep My Room Clean!

I cannot find anything when my room is a mess!
And when my room is a mess there is no place to rest!
And yucky things can hide there like rats and pests!
When in my room there is a big mess!
So I must keep it tidy!
I must keep it clean!
I must remember! That I am a Heavenly being!
I am a child of God!
And God wants me to be clean!
So I must remember to keep my room clean!

I Have To Study Hard!

I have to study hard!
So that when I grow up!
I can make lots of money!
And look after mummy and daddy!
I have to study hard!
So that when I grow up!
I can fix all the problems that the adults made!
I have to study hard!
So that when grow up!
I can support my wife and all my children!
I have to study hard!
So that when I grow up!
I can make the world better for everyone!

When I Grow Up I'm Going To Be A Man!

When I grow up I'm going to be a man!
And I'm going to follow Heavenly Fathers plan!
I'm going to be strong and do all that I can,
To be a good husband, to be a mighty Man!
I will love my wife with all my heart!
I will hug and kiss her everyday!
I will go to work and then come home and play!
With all of our children everyday!
Gods commandments I will teach them to obey!

And that when we have problems we should kneel down and pray!
For loving Heavenly Father to show to us the way!
I know that if I do this I will be ok!
I cannot wait to be a man!
I will practice now Everyday!
Heavenly Fathers Great Plan!

I Want To Be Like Jesus!

I want to be like Jesus!
He is so kind!
He fed 5000 people!
And didn't ask for a dime!
I want to be like Jesus!
He is so Mighty!
He shouted at the storm!
And calmed the sea!
I want to be like Jesus!
He loves us so much!
He made the blind man see!
I want to be like Jesus!
I will pay attention when I go to church!
So I will be like Jesus one day!

More to come!

The Hairless Monkeys

The Mating Behaviour of the Rhesus Monkey

While alpha males do their best to monopolise the group
and keep the females for themselves, females like to
counteract this strategy with secret sex and promiscuity.

———— ∿∾◦◖◦◗◦∿ ————

Arrogantly Assumptive

These are a crazy bunch who like to think,
Just because they show some skin,
Any man's heart they can win.
They can usually be spotted in the Jungles of Babylon,
Eating, drinking, being merry and indulging in sin.
Comparing their trophies from their pig hunts,
Just to see who wins.

And, behold, there met him a woman with the
attire of an harlot, and subtle of heart.
She is loud and stubborn, her feet abide not in her house.
Now is she without, now in the streets, and
lieth in wait at every corner.
So she caught him, and kissed him, and with
an impudent face said unto him,
I have peace offerings with me, this day have I payed my vows.
Therefore came I forth to meet thee diligently
to seek thy face and I have found thee.

I have decked my bed with coverings of tapestry,
with carved works, with fine linen of Egypt.
I have perfumed my bed with myrrh, aloes, and cinnamon.
Come, let us take our fill of love until the morning,
let us solace ourselves with loves.
For the goodman is not at home, he is gone a long journey.
He hath taken a bag of money with him, and
will come home at the day appointed.
With her much fair speech she caused him to yield,
with the flattering of her lips she forced him.
He goeth after her straightway, as an ox goeth to the
slaughter, or as a fool to the correction of the stocks.
Till a dart strike through his liver as a bird hasteth to
the snare, and knoweth not that it is for his life.
Hearken unto me now therefore O ye children,
and attend to the words of my mouth.
Let not thine heart decline to her ways, go not astray in her paths.
For she hath cast down many wounded, yea,
many strong men have been slain by her.
Her house is the way to hell, going down to the chambers of death.
Proverbs 7:10-27

The Female Monkey

With one man she never stays,
Instead with many she likes to play.
Her heart is stone and her love all gone,
All that remains is hollow lust,
And a need to feed has become a must.

A family life she does not want,
Her heart is self serving,
Rather she seeks after wild, riotous gatherings,
Where buffets of sin are serving.
Of a good man's heart she is undeserving.

For a whore is a deep ditch; and a strange woman is a narrow pit.
She also lieth in wait as for a prey, and increaseth
the transgressors among men.
Proverbs 23:27-28

———————

Unrefined

Just like the monkey they like to shout and scream!
Over matters of little consequence they will create a scene.
Stubborn and loud! Shameless and proud!
They have dangerous mouths that like to tell lies and shout false cries!
They dig pits to ensnare their prey,
Leading good men from their God away.

It is better to dwell in the corner of the housetop, than
with a brawling woman and in a wide house.
Proverbs 25:24

Let thy fountain be blessed: and rejoice with the wife of thy youth.
Let her be as the loving hind and pleasant roe; let her breasts satisfy
thee at all times; and be thou ravished always with her love.

And why wilt thou, my son, be ravished with a strange
woman, and embrace the bosom of a stranger?
Proverbs 5:18-20

The Poor Monkeys

The prevailing fashion among the Hairless Monkeys is immodesty,
They dress this way with hopes of attracting a nice guy,
But sadly the only thing they catch are flies,
That do deceive them with flattery and lies.
With only one thing on their minds these flies don't often stay,
Instead they will prey on the next Hairless
monkey that comes their way.
Why not come and learn the ways above,
Where together with the one you love,
Can be sealed together forever with Eternal Love,
And be showered with blessings from above.
Do not settle for less,
You are daughters of God,
And deserve nothing but the best.
Come to Gods church!
And in him you will find rest.